in
Cantonese

廣州話指南
Gwóngjàuwá
jínàahm

Kwan Choi Wah

THE COMMERCIAL PRESS

painting and calligraphy on the cover
ZHOU WAI MIN

廣州話指南
THE RIGHT WORD IN CANTONESE
Compiled by Kwan Choi Wah 關彩華

Published by
THE COMMERCIAL PRESS (HONG KONG) LTD.
Kiu Ying Bldg., 2D Finnie St., Quarry Bay, H.K.

Printed by
Elegance Printing & Book Binding Co., Ltd.
Block B1, 4/F., Hoi Bun Ind. Bldg.,
6 Wing Yip St., Kwun Tong, Kowloon, Hong Kong.

First Edition May 1989
Eighth Printing February 1995
ISBN 962 07 1106 8
Printed in Hong Kong

This book

is dedicated to all my students of Cantonese over the years, whose determination to learn the language often touched me and made me proud to be a language teacher.

I wish them success.

PREFACE

This book is designed to serve as a dictionary for students of Cantonese and as a handbook for visitors to Hong Kong. For students of Cantonese, I hope this book will be useful in expanding their vocabulary. For those living in Hong Kong, I hope they will find the vocabulary relevant and most practical in their daily life. Visitors, I hope will look up a word, pronounce it in Cantonese and thus make an attempt to communicate with the local people. Or, if this fails, they can simply show the entry, with characters, to the people they are trying to communicate with.

There are two parts in the book with a total of 7500 entries. Part one consists of everyday vocabulary. Part two consists of specialized glossaries with special reference to Hong Kong.

The English entries are followed by "Yale Romanizations," a system to teach students to pronounce Cantonese sounds and characters. Generally the entries follow this pattern: English — Cantonese — Character. The English entries are in alphabetical order. Some characters used in this book are not the traditional characters in Chinese writing. I call them Cantonese characters and they are used in putting Cantonese, one of the spoken dialects of Chinese, into written form. Therefore, it is necessary to note that not every Cantonese sound has a character in written form. (I use the sign □ to indicate such cases.) The reason for having characters in the book is the hope that they will make it easier for students or visitors to get help from their Cantonese friends in pronouncing the sounds more accurately. Most Cantonese speakers do not know much about romanization systems.

Many people have contributed to this book in one way or another. My special thanks are due to Ms. Mary

Ann Ganey, Brother Patrick Tierney, Miss Joyce Shiu, Mr. Donald Keesee and the staff of Commercial Press for their information, criticism, advice, corrections, typing and editing. I am particuarly grateful to my parents, friends and students for much-needed encouragement while this book was in preparation. To Mr. Zhou Wai Min of Beijing, goes special thanks for this painting and calligraphy on the cover of this book.

The errors and shortcomings of the book should be attributed solely to me. Suggestions for improvement will be deeply appreciated, and may be sent to me at: New Asia — Yale-in-China Chinese Language Centre, The Chinese University of Hong Kong, Shatin, New Territories, Hong Kong.

關彩華

Introduction to Cantonese Pronunciation

There are several romanization systems used in Teaching Cantonese to non-Chinese speakers. The system used in this book is the Yale system.

A syllable in Cantonese is made up of three elements:

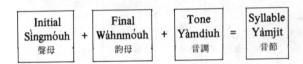

An initial is the beginning consonant(s) of the syllable. A final is the vowel(s) and consonant(s) that follow the initial in the syllable. A tone is the pitch contour of the syllable. In the Yale system there are 19 initials, 51 finals and 7 tones.

Initials

The 19 initials are: B, CH, D, F, G, GW, H, J, K, KW, L, M, N, NG, P, S, T, W, Y. According to the articulation, they can be grouped into aspirated stops, non-aspirated stops, nasals, fricative and continuants, and semi-vowels.

The 19 initials in Cantonese

Articulation	Symbol	IPA	Key Word	
Aspirated stops	P	P'	pàh	爬
	T	T'	tà	他
	K	K'	kà	卡
	CH	TS'	chà	叉
	KW	KW	kwà	誇
Non-aspirated stops	B	P	bà	爸
	D	T	dá	打
	G	K	gà	家
	J	TS	jà	渣
	GW	KW	gwa	掛
Nasals	M	M	mà	媽
	N	N	nàh	拿
	NG	ŋ	ngàh	牙
Fricative and continuants	F	F	fa	化
	L	L	lā	啦
	H	H	hà	蝦
	S	ʃ	sá	灑
Semi-vowels	Y	J	yáh	也
	W	W	wàh	華

Finals

In pronouncing the finals in Cantonese, the following points should be noted; First, the vowel length in the finals may be long or short and this affects the pronounciation of the syllable. A long vowel has a weak ending as in "sàam 三 ", "gàai 街 ", while a short vowel has a strong ending as in "gai 計 ", "sàm 心 ". Second, final endings *p, t, k* are not aspirated. Third, finals starting with *eu, u* and *yu* are pronounced with rounded lips.

The 51 finals in Cantonese

Finals Starting with	Vowel Length Long	Key Word				Vowel Length Short	Key Word			
		Initial	Final	Tone	in Character		Initial	Final	Tone	in Character
"A"	a	p	a	M.L.	怕	ai	g	ai	M.L.	計
	aai	d	aai	M.L.	帶	au	t	àu	H.F.	偷
	aau	g	àau	H.F.	交	am	s	àm	H.F.	心
	aam	ch	áam	H.R.	慘	an	m	ahn	L.L.	問
	aan	s	àan	H.F.	山	ang	d	áng	H.R.	等
	aang	t	àahng	L.F.	彈	ap	j	àp	H.F.	執
	aap	g	aap	M.L.	甲	at	ch	āt	H.L.	七
	aat	b	aat	M.L.	八	ak	d	ahk	L.L.	特
	aak	j	aahk	L.L.	摘					
"E"	e	j	e	M.L.	借	ei	m	éih	L.R.	美
	eng	l	eng	M.L.	靚					
	ek	s	ehk	L.L.	石					
"EU"	eu	h	èu	H.F.	靴	eui	g	eui	M.L.	句
	eung	ch	ēung	H.L.	窗	eun	j	ēun	H.L.	椿
	euk	g	euk	M.L.	腳	eut	ch	ēut	H.L.	出
"I"	i	j	ì	H.F.	知	ing	m	ìhng	L.F.	明
	iu	y	ìu	M.L.	要	ik	s	ihk	L.L.	食
	im	s	ìm	H.R.	閃					
	in	t	ìn	H.F.	天					
	ip	g	ip	M.L.	劫					
	it	d	it	M.L.	跌					
"O"	o	g	ō	H.L.	歌	ou	l	óuh	L.R.	老
	oi	t	ói	H.R.	柏					
	on	ng	òn	H.F.	安					
	ong	m	ohng	L.L.	望					
	ot	h	ot	M.L.	喝					
	ok	gw	ok	M.L.	國					
"U"	u	g	ù	H.F.	姑	ung	j	ùhg	H.F.	鐘
	ui	f	ùi	H.F.	灰	uk	d	unk	L.L.	讀
	un	w	uhn	L.L.	換					
	ut	f	ut	M.L.	闊					
"YU"	yu	j	yù	H.F.	珠					
	yun	ch	yùn	H.F.	穿					
	yut	s	yut	M.L.	雪					

Tones

There are 7 tones in Cantonese with three main contours: falling, rising and level, which are distinguished by using diacritics/tone marks on top of the first vowel in the final.

The 7 tones are: High falling, high rising, mid level, high level, low falling, low rising and low level, when spelling, *h* is inserted after the vowel(s) of the final to indicate low tones and is not voiced.

Below is a diagram of the tones in Cantonese.

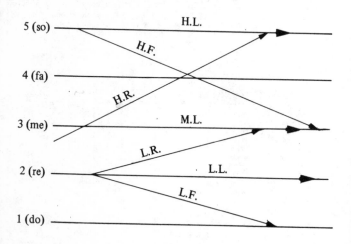

The following chart will clarify tone usage:

	Tone	H.F.	H.R.	M.L.	H.L.	L.F.	L.R.	L.L.
Word	in symbol	sì	sí	si	sī	sìh	síh	sih
	in character	施	史	試	詩	時	市	是
	in symbol	mà	má	ma	mā	màh	máh	mah
	in character	媽			嗎	嘛	馬	騙
Key	in symbol	chèung	chéung	cheung	chēung	chèuhng	chéuhng	cheuhng
	in character	搶	搶	唱	窗	詳		
	in symbol	sàm	sám	sam	sām	sàhm	sáhm	sahm
	in character	心	審	滲	深	岑		甚
	in symbol	fàn	fán	fan	fān	fàhn	fáhn	fahn
	in character	分	粉	訓	芬	墳	奮	份

Comparative Chart of
Four Romanization Systems

INITIALS

YALE	IPA	SIDNEY LAU	MEYER-WEMPE
P	P'	P	P'
B	P	B	P
T	T'	T	T'
D	T	D	T
K	K'	K	K'
G	K	G	K
CH	Tʃ'	CH	CH', TS'
J	Tʃ	J	CH, TS
KW	K'W	KW	K'W
GW	KW	GW	KW
M	M	M	M
N	N	N	N
NG	ŋ	NG	NG
F	F	F	F
L	L	L	L
H	H	H	H
S	ʃ	S	S, SH
Y	J	Y	I, Y
W	W	W	OO, W

FINALS

YALE	IPA	SIDNEY LAU	MEYER-WEMPE
A	A:	A	A
AAI	A:I	AAI	AAI
AAU	A:U	AAU	AAU
AAM	A:M	AAM	AAM
AAP	A:P	AAP	AAP
AAN	A:N	AAN	AAN
AAT	A:T	AAT	AAT
AANG	A:ŋ	AANG	AANG
AAK	A:K	AAK	AAK
AI	AI	AI	AI
AU	AU	AU	AU
AM	AM	AM	AM, OM

AP	AP	AP	AP, OP
AN	AN	AN	AN
AT	AT	AT	AT
ANG	AŊ	ANG	ANG
AK	AK	AK	AK
E	ɛ:	E	E
ENG	ɛ: ŋ	ENG	ENG
EK	ɛ: K	EK	EK
EI	EI	EI	EI
EU	OE:	EUH	OEH
EUNG	ɔE:ŋ	EUNG	EUNG
EUK	OE:K	EUK	EUK
EUI	OEI	UI	UI
EUN	OEN	UN	UN
EUT	OET	UT	UT
I	I:	I	I
IU	I:U	IU	IU
IM	I:M	IM	IM
IP	I:P	IP	IP
IN	I:ŋ	IN	IN
IT	I:T	IT	IT
ING	I ŋ	ING	ING
IK	IK	IK	IK
O	O	OH	OH
OI	O:I	OI	OI
ON	O:N	ON	ON
OT	O:T	OT	OT
ONG	O:ŋ	ONG	ONG
OK	O:K	OK	OK
OU	OU	O	O
U	U	OO	OO
UI	U:I	OOI	OOI
UN	U:N	OON	OON
UT	U:T	OOT	OOT
UNG	U:ŋ	UNG	UNG
UK	U:K	UK	UK
YU	Y:	UE	UE
YUN	Y:N	UEN	UEN
YUT	Y:T	UET	UET

TONES

YALE		SIDNEY LAU		MEYER-WEMPE	
HIGH FALLING	À	HIGH FALLING 1	A^1	UPPER EVEN	A
HIGH RISING	Á	MIDDLE RISING 2	A^2	UPPER RISING	Á
MIDDLE LEVEL	A, AT	MIDDLE LEVEL 3	A^3	UPPER GOING / MIDDLE ENTERING	Â / ÂT
HIGH LEVEL	Ā, ĀT	HIGH LEVEL 1°	$A^{1°}$	UPPER EVEN / UPPER ENTERING	A / AT
LOW FALLING	ÀH	LOW FALLING 4	A^4	LOW EVEN	Ā
LOW RISING	ÁH	LOW RISING 5	A^5	LOWER RISING	Ǎ
LOW LEVEL	AH, AHT	LOW LEVEL 6	A^6	LOWER GOING / LOWER ENTERING	Â / ÂT

Contents

Preface i

Introduction to Cantonese Pronunciation iii

Part I: Everyday Vocabulary 1–127

Part II: Specialized Glossaries, with special Reference
      to Hong Kong

  1. *Where to go in Hong Kong* 129
      Names of Places 129
      Beaches and Bays 131
      Outlying Islands 131
      Country Parks 132
      Reservoirs 132
  2. *How to get there* 134
      Transportation 134
      MTR and KCR Stations 138
  3. *What to do* 141
      Recreation and Sports 141
      Museums 157
      Public Amenities 158
      Fine Arts 158
      Places of Interest 159
      Cinemas 160
      Chinese Musical Instruments 160
  4. *What to eat and drink* 162
      Food 162
      Basic Seasonings and Ingredients for Chinese
        Cooking. 164
      Cantonese Dishes 165
      Chinese Tea 168
      Cooking Methods 169
      Dim-Sum 169
      Drinks 172
      Fruits 174

    Kitchen Utensils 175
    Noodle and Rice 177
    Seafood 181
    Vegetables 182
5. *Where to get help if you are sick* 184
    Medical Service and Health Terminology 184
    Hospitals 190
    Parts of the Body 192
6. *How to plan for a trip* 196
    Air Lines Companies 196
    Banks 198
    Hotels and Guest Houses 198
    Major Cities in China 200
    Major Cities in the World 201
7. *How to find out what's happening* 205
    Mass Media 205
    Magazines 209
    News Agency 210
    Newspapers 210
    TV Stations, Radio Stations 211
8. *How Hong Kong is run* 212
    Government Departments and Secretariat 212
9. *Where to worship in Hong Kong* 217
    Churches and Temples 217
10. *How education is conducted* 219

Appendices:

1. Family relations 232
2. "Loanwords" in Cantonese 236
3. Twelve animal signs of the Chinese Zodiac 239

Part I

Everyday Vocabulary

A

a dozen	yāt dā	一打
a kind of	yeuhng	樣
a little dizzy	wàhnwándéi	暈暈地
a little, a few	yāt dī	一啲
a tiny bit (a small portion)	dīgamdēu, dītgamdēu, dīkgamdēu, dīkgamdō	啲咁多
A.D. (anno domini)	géiyùhnhauh	紀元後
abacus	syunpùhn	算盤
abalone	bāauyùh	鮑魚
abandon	fonghei	放棄
Aberdeen	Hèunggóngjái	香港仔
ability	nàhnglihk, búnsih	能力，本事
ablaze (with brilliant lights)	dāngfó fāiwòhng	燈火輝煌
able	hóyíh, nàhnggau	可以，能夠
able to tell	táidākchēut	睇得出
abnormal	m̀jingsèuhng	唔正常
abortion	dohtòi	墮胎
about to	jèunggahn, jèunggán	將近
about, concerning	gwàanyù	關於
above a certain number or grade	... yíhseuhng	……以上
abrasion	syún	損
absolute	jyuhtdeui	絕對
abundant, rich	fùngfu	豐富
academic	hohkseuht	學術
accent (spoken)	háuyām	口音
accept	jipsauh	接受
accident	yi ngoih, sātsih	意外，失事
accidentally	ngáuhyìhn	偶然
accommodate (for charity)	sàuyùhng	收容

1

accommodate	yùhngnaahp	容納
accompany	pùih	陪
accomplish, complete	yùhnsìhng	完成
according to	jiu, yijiu	照，依照
account in a bank	wuhháu	戶口
accountant	wuihgaisī, wuihgai	會計師，會計
accurate (pronunciation)	jeng	正
accustomed to	gwaan	慣
acheivement	sìhngjauh, sìhngjīk	成就，成績
act, as an actor	jouhhei	做戲
action	hàhngduhng	行動
active, lively	wuhtput	活潑
activities	wuhtduhng	活動
actually	kèihsaht	其實
acupuncture	jàmgau	針灸
acute disease	gāpjing	急症
add to, increase	jānggā	增加
address	deihji	地址
address (with proper title)	chìngfù	稱呼
adhere	chi	黐.
administration	hàhngjing	行政
administrator	hàhngjingyàhnyùhn	行政人員
admire	puifuhk, yànséung	佩服，欣賞
adult	daaihyàhn	大人
adult education	sìhngyàhn gaauyuhk	成人教育
adversity	waahnnaahn	患難
advertisement	goubaahk, gwónggou	告白，廣告
advertising company	gwónggougùngsi	廣告公司
advise, persuade	hyun	勸
advocate, suggest	jyújèung	主張
aerogram	yàuh gáan	郵簡
affable, kind	hóusèungyúh, hóuyàhnsí	好相與，好人事

2

affairs, matter	sihchìhng	事情
afraid	gèng	驚
Africa	Fèi jàu	非洲
after ...	...jìhauh	……之後
after all	gaujíng, doudái	究竟，到底
afternoon	hahjau	下晝
afternoon nap	ngaan gaau	晏覺
afternoon tea	hahnǵhchàh	下午茶
afterwards, later on	hauhlòih, sāumēi	後來，收尾
afterwards, then	yìhnhauh	然後
again	yauh	又
again, once more	joi	再
age	nìhngéi	年紀
agent, be agent	doihléih	代理
ago	...jìchìhn	……之前
agriculture	nùhngyihp	農業
Aids	ngoijībehng	愛滋病
aim at	ji joih	志在
aim, object, goal	muhkdīk	目的
air	hùnghei	空氣
air force	hùnggwàn	空軍
air hostess	hùngjùng siujé	空中小姐
air-conditioner	láahngheigēi	冷氣機
air-conditioning	láahnghei	冷氣
air-line company	hòhnghùng gūngsī	航空公司
aircraft-carrier	hòhnghùngmóuhlaahm	航空母艦
airmail letter	hòhnghùngseun	航空信
airplane	fèigèi	飛機
airport, airfield	(fèi) gèichèuhng	（飛）機場
alas!	séi lo!	死咯！
all	tùngtùng, sóyáuhge	通通，所有嘅
all around	seiwàih	四圍
all of a sudden	dahtyìhngāan, dahkyìhngāan	突然間
all the time	jàusìh	周時
allergic, allergy	máhngám	敏感

allocate	buht	撥
allow	jéun, béi	准，俾
Alma Mater	móuhhaauh	母校
almost, hardly	gèifùh	幾乎
almost, nearly	chābātdō, chāmdō	差不多，差唔多
alphabet	jihmóuh	字母
already	yìhgìng	已經
also, as well	dōu, yihkdōu	都，亦都
alter, correct	gói	改
although	sèuiyìhn	雖然
altogether	hahmbaahnglaahng	冚唪呤
altruistic	waihyàhn	爲人
aluminium pot	tāibōu	鋁煲
alumni association	haauhyáuhwúi	校友會
always	sìhsìh dōu	時時都
ambassador	daaihsi	大使
ambition	yéhsàm, jihei	野心，志氣
ambitious	gaujihei	夠志氣
ambulance	gausēungchè	救傷車
ambulance corps	gausēungdéui	救傷隊
America	méihjàu	美洲
America (U.S.A.)	Méihgwok	美國
among	kèihjùng	其中
amusing, enjoyable	hóuwáan	好玩
anaemia	pàhnhyut	貧血
anaesthetic	màhjeuiyeuhk	麻醉藥
anaesthetist	màhjeuisī	麻醉師
ancestor	jóusìn	祖先
ancestral hall	chìhtòhng	祠堂
ancient times	gúdoih, gúsìh	古代，古時
and	tùhng	同
and so on, etc.	dángdáng	等等
angel	tìnsi	天使
angry	nàu	嬲

4

animal	duhngmaht	動物
ankle	geukngáahn	脚眼
annual ball	jàunìhnmóuhwúi	週年舞會
annual meeting	jàunìhndaaihwúi	週年大會
another	daihyih	第二
another one	lìhngngoih yātgo	另外一個
answer (v)	daap	答
antiques, curio	gúdúng, gúwún	古董，古玩
any time	chèuihsìh	隨時
anyway, anyhow	wàahngdihm	橫掂
apartment building	daaihhah	大廈
apathetic	láahngdaahm	冷淡
apologize	douhhip	道歉
appearance, features	yéung	樣
appendicitis	màahngchéungyìhm	盲腸炎
appendix (of a book)	fuhluhk	附錄
appetite	waihháu	胃口
applaud	paaksáu	拍手
apple	pìhnggwó	蘋果
appliances, tools	yuhnggeuih	用具
application form	sànchíngbíu	申請表
apply	sànchíng	申請
apply lipstick	chàh sèuhngòu	搽唇膏
apply on, put on	chàh	搽
apply powder	chàhfán	搽粉
appreciate (of a favor)	gámgīk	感激
apprentice	hohktòuh, tòuhdái	學徒，徒弟
approximately, about	yeukmók ..., ... jóyáu	約莫，左右
apricot	hahng	杏
April	Seiyuht	四月
apron	wàihkwán	圍裙

5

architect	(waahk) jīksì	（畫）則師
area (location)	deihkèui	地區
area (measurement for a place)	mihnjīk	面積
argue	ngaaugéng	拗頸
arm	sáubei	手臂
armed forces	gwàndéui	軍隊
army	luhkgwàn	陸軍
aroma	hèungmeih	香味
arouse	yáhnhéi	引起
arrange (things in a place)	bouji	佈置
arrange, display	báai	擺
arrange, dispose	ngònpàaih, chyúléih	安排，處理
arrest	làai	拉
arrive, reach	dou	到
art	ngaihseuht	藝術
artificial	yàhnjouh, gá	人造，假
artist	ngaihseuhtgā	藝術家
as far as I know	jiu ngóh sójì	照我所知
as if, seems	chíhfùh	似乎
as much (many) as possible	jeuhnleuhng	盡量
as one pleases, whatever one likes	chèuih . . . jùngyi lā, chèuih (bín) . . . lā	隨…中意啦，隨(便)……啦
as soon as possible	jeuhnfaai	盡快
as to, as for	jiyù	至於
ascend	sing	升
ash	fùi	灰
ash tray	yīnfùidip	烟灰碟
Asia	Ngajàu	亞洲
ask	mahn	問
ask after, send regards to	mahnhauh	問候
ask for a leave	chéngga, gouga	請假，告假

6

ask for advice (polite form)	chénggaau	請教
ask for directions	mahnlouh	問路
askew, not straight	mé	歪
Aspro	Asihbātlòh	亞士匹羅
assistant	johsáu, bòngsáu	助手，幫手
assorted fruit	jaahpgwó	雜果
astigmatism	sáangwòng	散光
astronaut	taaihùngyàhn	太空人
astronomer	tinmàhnhohkgā	天文學家
astronomy	tinmàhn	天文
at any time, any moment	chèuihsìh	隨時
at dark	tin hàak	天黑
at daybreak	tin gwòng	天光
at present	muhkchìhn	目前
at that time, at that moment	gójahnsì, dòngsìh	嗰陣時，當時
at the same time	tùhngsìh	同時
at the time of ..	... gójahnsì	……嗰陣時
attitude	taaidouh	態度
attorney	leuhtsī	律師
attractive	leng	靚
audience	tingjung	聽眾
audience, spectators	gùnjung	觀眾
auditorium	láihtòhng	禮堂
August	Baatyuht	八月
Australia	Ngoujàu, Oujàu	澳洲
author	jokjé, jokgā	作者，作家
autobiography	jihjyún	自傳
automatic	jihduhng	自動
automobile, car	chè, heichè	車，汽車
autumn	chàutin	秋天

7

avail oneself of an opportunity	je nīgo gēiwuih	借呢個機會
average	pìhnggwàn	平均
average grade	pìhnggwànfàn	平均分
aviation	hòhnghùng	航空
avoid	beihhòi, beihmihn	避開，避免
awakened (by noise)	chòuhséng	嘈醒
axe	fútáu	斧頭
azalea	douhgyūnfā	杜鵑花

B

B.A. or B.S.	hohksih	學士
B.C. (before Christ)	géiyùhnchìhn	紀元前
baby	bìhbījái	啤啤仔
back (of the body)	buijek	背脊
back door	hauhmún	後門
back up	tanhauh	褪後
background	buiging	背景
bacon	yīnyuhk	烟肉
bad	waaih	壞
bag	dói	袋
baggage, luggage	hàhngléih	行李
bake	guhk	焗
balcony	kèhláu	騎樓
ball	bō, kàuh	波，球
ball-pen	yùhnjíbāt	原子筆
ballet	bālèuihmóuh	芭蕾舞
ballroom	móuhtèng	舞廳
bamboo	jūk	竹
bamboo scaffolding	jūkpàahng	竹棚
banana	hèungjiu	香蕉

8

band	ngohkdéui	樂隊
bandage (n)	bāngdáai	硼帶
bandage (v)	bāaujaat	包紮
bank	ngàhnhòhng	銀行
bankrupt	pocháan	破產
banquet	yinwuih	宴會
bar, pub	jáubā	酒吧
barber shop	fèifaatpóu	飛髮鋪
bargain	góngga	講價
bargirl	bānéui	吧女
bark (n)	syuhpèih	樹皮
bark (v)	faih	吠
base on (upon)	gàngeui	根據
baseball	lèuihkàuh	壘球
basement, cellar	deihlòuh	地牢
basic, basis	gànbún, gèichó	根本，基礎
basically	gànbúnseuhng	根本上
basin, pot	pùhn	盆
basket	láam	籃
basketball	làahmkàuh	籃球
bath towel	mòuhgàn	毛巾
bath-robe	yuhkpòuh	浴袍
bath-tub	yuhkgōng	浴缸
bathing suit	wihngyī	泳衣
bathroom, shower	chùnglèuhngfóng	冲涼房
battery	dihnsām	電心
battery (for car)	dihnchìh	電池
bay	hóiwāan	海灣
be (a doctor, teacher, etc.)	jouh	做
be expert experienced	joihhòhng, yáuhgìngyihm	在行，有經驗
be named, be called by	giu, giujouh	叫，叫做
be sure to	jigán	至緊
be touching	lihng yàhn gámduhng	令人感動
beach	sātāan	沙灘

9

bean curd	dauhfuh	豆腐
beans	dáu	豆
bear, stand	yán	忍
beard	sōu, wùh sòu	鬚，鬍鬚
beat, hit	dá	打
beat, win	yèhng	贏
beautiful	leng	靚
because	yànwaih	因為
because of, due to	yàuhyù	由於
become, change into	binsèhng	變成
become rich	faatdaaht	發達
bed	chòhng	床
bed room	seuihfóng	睡房
bed spread	chòhngkám	床冚
bee	mahtfùng	蜜蜂
beef	ngàuhyuhk	牛肉
beef steak	ngàuhpá	牛扒
beer	bējáu	啤酒
before, formerly	yihchìhn	以前
beforehand, in advance	sihsìn, yuhsìn	事先，預先
beg	kàuh	求
begger	hātyī	乞兒
begin, commence	hòichí	開始
behind	hái . . . hauhmihn	喺……後面
beige	máihsīk	米色
believe	sèungseun, seun	相信，信
believe (in a religion)	seungaau	信教
believe it or not	seun bāt seun yàuh néih	信不信由你
bell	jūng	鐘
belly, stomach	tóuh	肚
belong to	suhkyù	屬於

below a certain number or grade	... yìhhah	……以下
belt	pèihdáai	皮帶
bench	chèuhngdang	長凳
beneficial, conductive	yáuhyīk, yáuhyīkchyu	有益，有益處
benefit, interest	leihyīk	利益
beside, next to	pòhngbīn	旁邊
besides, more-over	yihché	而且
besides, the other	lihngngoih	另外
best man	buhnlóng	伴郎
bet	syùdóu	輸賭
between..., among...	... jigàan	……之間
beware of	dōngsàm	當心
bib	háuséuigìn	口水肩
Bible	Singgìng	聖經
bicycle	dāanchè	單車
big	daaih	大
biology	sāngmaht (hohk)	生物（學）
bird	jéuk, jeukjái	雀，雀仔
birth control	jityuhk	節育
birthday	sàangyaht	生日
birthday card	sàangyaht kāat	生日咭
birthday gift	sàangyaht láihmaht	生日禮物
biscuit	bénggòn	餅乾
bite (v)	ngáauh	咬
bitter	fú	苦
black	hāak	黑
black-and-white	hāakbaahk	黑白
black coffee	jāaifē	齋啡
blackboard	hāakbáan	黑板
bladder	pòhnggwòng	膀胱
blame	gwaai	怪
blanket	jīn, péih	氈，被

bleach	piubaahk	漂白
bleed	làuhhyut	流血
bless	bóuyauh, jūkfūk	保佑，祝福
blessings	hahngfūk	幸福
blind	màahng(ngáahn)	盲（眼）
blood	hyut	血
blood brothers	chànhingdaih	親兄弟
blood pressure	hyutngaat	血壓
blood test	yihmhyut	驗血
blood transfusion	syùhyut	輸血
blouse	(néuihjòng) sēutsāam	（女裝）恤衫
blow	chèui	吹
blue (color)	làahmsīk, làahm	藍色，藍
boarding card	dānggèijing	登機證
boarding student	geisūksāng	寄宿生
boat, ship	syùhn	船
body	sàntái	身體
boil (n)	chōng	瘡
boil (v)	bōu	煲
boiled water	gwán séui	滾水
bone	gwāt	骨
book	syù	書
book case	syùgwaih	書柜
book shelf	syùgá	書架
bookstore	syùpóu, syùdim	書舖，書店
boot	hēu	靴
boring	muhn	悶
born	chēutsai	出世
borrow	je	借
bortsch	lòhsung tòng	羅宋湯
boss, proprietor	sihtáu, lóuhbáan	事頭，老板
bothersome	faisih	費事
bottle	jēun	樽
bow of a vessel	syùhntàuh	船頭
bow tie	bōutāai	〔煲〕呔
bowl	wún	碗

box	háp, sēung	盒，箱
boy	nàahmjái	男仔
bracelet	ngáak	鈪
brain	nóuh (gàn)	腦（筋）
brake, switch	jai	掣
branch of a bank or firm	fànhóng, fāngūngsì	分行，分公司
brand-name	pàaih(jí)	牌（子）
Brandy	Baahklāandéi	白蘭地
brassiere	hùngwàih	胸圍
bread	mihnbāau	麵包
break (v)	jínglaahn, dálaahn	整爛，打爛
breake (v)	saat jai	利掣
breakfast	jóuchāan	早餐
breast	hùng, sàmháu	胸，心口
breast-feeding	sihk yàhnnáaih	食人奶
breathe	táuhei, fūkāp	唞氣，呼吸
bribe	kúilouh	賄賂
bride	sànnéung	新娘
bride's family	néuihgā	女家
bridegroom	sànlóng, sànlòhnggō	新郎，新郎哥
bridegroom's family	nàahmgā	男家
bridesmaid	buhnnéung	伴娘
bridge	kìuh	橋
brief case	gùngsihbāau	公事包
bright	gwòng (máahng)	光（猛）
broadcast	gwóngbo	廣播
broken (into two parts)	tyúhn	斷
broken, rotten	laahn	爛
broker	gìnggéi	經紀
bronchitis	jiheigúnyìhm	支氣管炎
bronze statue	tùhngjeuhng	銅像
broom	soubá	掃把
brothers	hingdaih	兄弟

brown	gafēsīk	咖啡色
brown sugar	wòhngtòhng	黃糖
bruise	yú	瘀
brush	sóu, cháat	掃、擦
brush one's teeth	chaatngàh	擦牙
bucket, barrel	túng	桶
Buddhist, Buddhism	Fahtgaau	佛教
budget	yuhsyun	預算
buffet	jihjoh chāan	自助餐
build	héi	起
building	láu	樓
bully, take advantage	hà	蝦
bump into (persons etc.), collide (cars)	johng	撞
burn, put fire to	sìu	燒
burnt (overcook)	jyúlūng	煮燶
bury	jong	葬
bus	bāsí	巴士
bus lane	bāsí jyūnsin	巴士專線
business administration	gùngsèung-gúnléih	工商管理
business of an organization	yihpmouh	業務
business trade	sàangyi	生意
bustling	yihtnaauh	熱鬧
busy (not free)	m̀dākhàahn	唔得閑
but, however	daahnhaih	但係
butter	ngàuhyàuh	牛油
butterfly	wùhdíp	蝴蝶
button	náu	鈕
button up	kaunáu	扣鈕
buy	máaih	買
buy groceries	máaihsung	買餸

14

by (bus, boat)	daap	搭
by all means, be sure	chinkèih	千祈
by coincidence	ngāamngāam	啱啱
by that time	dousih	到時
by the way	gónghéi séuhnglàih	講起上嚟

C

cabin (in a ship)	syùhnchòng	船艙
cable car	laahmchè	纜車
cake	béng	餅
calculate, figure out	gai	計
calendar	yahtlihk	日曆
call, ask	giu	叫
call, to be called	giujouh	叫做
calm, still	pihngjihng	平靜
calm, undisturbed	jandihng, daahmdihng	鎮定，啖定
camera	(yíng)séunggèi	（影）相機
can (know how to), be able to	wúih	會
can, may	hóyíh	可以
can-opener	guntáudōu	罐頭刀
can't help but	yánm̀jyuh	忍唔住
Canada	Gānàhdaaih	加拿大
canal	wahnhòh	運河
cancer	ngàahm, kēngsá	癌；□□
candle	laahpjūk	蠟燭
candlestick	jūktòih	燭台
candy	tóng	糖
canned food, can	guntáu	罐頭
cannot handle	yingfuh m̀làih	應付唔嚟
canteen	faahntòhng	飯堂

15

Cantonese (dialect)	Gwóngdùngwá, Gwóngjàuwá	廣東話, 廣州話
Cantonese opera	daaihhei, yuhtkeh	大戲,粵劇
cape (garment)	dáupùhng	斗蓬
capital (money)	búnchìhn, jīgàm	本錢,資金
capital (of a nation)	sáudōu	首都
capitalism	jibúnjyúyih	資本主義
captain (of a ship)	syùhnjéung	船長
car	chè	車
car accident	gāautùng yingoih	交通意外
car key	chèsih	車匙
carboard box	jíháp	紙盒
card	kāat	咭
care about, concern	gwàansàm	關心
career, enterprise	sihyihp	事業
careful, cautious	síusàm	小心
carnation	hōngnáaihhìng	康乃馨
carpenter	daumuhksìfú	鬥木師傅
carpentry	daumuhk	鬥木
carpet, rug	deihjīn	地氈
carry (as by vehicle)	joi	載
carry (under one's arm)	gihp	挾
carry between two or more persons	tòih	抬
carry on one's shoulder	dāam	擔
carry out	sahthàhng	實行
carve, carving	dìuhāk	雕刻
case	ngon gín, gongon	案件,個案
cash	yihnchìn, yihngām	現錢,現金
cashier	sàungányùhn	收銀員

casino	dóuchèuhng, dóugún	賭場，賭館
casual acquaintance	póutùng pàhngyáuh	普通朋友
casually	kàuhkèih	求其
cat	māau	貓
catalogue, list	muhkluhk	目錄
catch	jūk	捉
catch cold	láahngchàn	冷親
Catholic, Catholicism	Tìnjyúgaau	天主敎
catsup	kéjāp	茄汁
cattle	ngàuh	牛
catty	gàn	斤
cause	lihng	令
cavity	jyungàh	蛀牙
ceiling	tìnfābáan	天花板
celebrate	hingjūk	慶祝
celebrate the new year	gwonìhn	過年
cement	hùhngmòuhnàih	紅毛泥
cent	sīn	仙
center	jùngsàm	中心
century	saigéi	世紀
ceremony	yìhsīk	儀式
certainly, definitely	yātdihng, gáng	一定，梗
certainly, really	jànhaih	眞係
certificate, diploma	jingsyù, màhnpàhng	證書，文憑
certificate of stock	gúpiu	股票
chain	lín	鏈
chair	yí	椅
chairman	jyújihk	主席
champagne	hèungbàn (jáu)	香檳（酒）
champion	gungwān	冠軍
chance	gèiwuih	機會

change, alter	góibin	改變
change, exchange	wuhn	換
change, money in small unit	sáanngán	散銀
change a date	góikèih	改期
change address	gói deihjí	改地址
change another train, bus etc.	jyunchè	轉車
change clothes	wuhnsāam	換衫
chaos	wahnlyuhn	混亂
chapel, church	gaautòhng, láihbaaitòhng	教堂，禮拜堂
chapel, church (used by Catholics)	singtóng	聖堂
chapter (of book)	jēung	章
character (of a person)	singgaak	性格
characteristics	dahkdím	特點
charge by the month	on yuht gai	按月計
charity	chìhsihn	慈善
chart, drawing	tòuh	圖
chase, pursue	jèui	追
chase away	gón	趕
chat, converse	kìnggái	傾偈
cheap	pèhng	平
check	chēk, gimchàh	□，檢查，
cheek	mihn	面
cheese	chīsí, jisí	芝士
chef	chyùhsī, daaihchyú	廚師，大廚
chemistry	fahohk	化學
cheque	jípiu	支票
chest	sàmháu	心口
chicken	gāi	鷄
child	saimānjái, sailóugō	細蚊仔，細佬哥

18

children	saimānjái, siútuhng	細蚊仔，小童
chin	hahpàh	下巴
China	Jùnggwok	中國
China Mainland	Daaihluhk	大陸
Chinatown	Tòhngyàhngāai,	唐人街，
	Tòhngyàhnfauh	唐人埠
Chinese	Jùngmahn, Jùngmán	中文
(language)		
Chinese brush pen	mòuhbāt	毛筆
Chinese character	Jùnggwokjih	中國字
Chinese doctor	jùngyi	中醫
Chinese dress	tòhngjòng	唐裝
Chinese food	tòhngchāan, jùngchoi	唐餐，中菜
Chinese ink	mahk	墨
Chinese mushroom	dùnggù	冬菇
Chinese New	Nihnsāamsahpmáahn,	年三十晚，
Year's Eve	Nihnsā ahmáahn	年卅晚
Chinese style	kèihpóu, chèuhngsāam	旗袍，長衫
ladies' dress		
chocolate	jyūgùlīk	朱古力
cholera	foklyuhn	霍亂
chop, cut	jáam	斬
chop, stamp, seal	tòuhjēung, yan	圖章，印
chopper	choidōu	菜刀
chopping block	jāmbáan	砧板
chopsticks	faaiji	筷子
chorus	hahpcheungtyùhn	合唱團
Christ	Gēidūk	基督
Christian	Gēidūktòuh	基督徒
Christmas	Singdaanjit	聖誕節
Christmas card	singdaankāat	聖誕咭
Christmas carol	Singdaangō	聖誕歌
Christmas carol-	bougāaiyām	報佳音
ling		
Christmas Eve	Singdaan chìhnjihk	聖誕前夕
Christmas gift	Singdaan láihmaht	聖誕禮物
chrysanthemum	gūkfà	菊花

cicada, broad locust	sìhm	蟬
cigarette	yīn, yīnjái	烟，烟仔
cigarette ashes	yīnfūi	烟灰
cigarette butts	yīntáu	烟頭
cigarette-lighter	dáfógèi	打火機
circle (n)	yùhnhyūn	圓圈
circumstance, condition	chìhngyìhng	情形
circus	máhhei	馬戲
citizen	gùngmàhn	公民
city	sìhngsíh	城市
City Hall	Daaihwuihtòhng	大會堂
class (social)	gāaikāp	階級
class is over	lohktòhng	落堂
classic music	gúdin yamngohk	古典音樂
classmate	tùhnghohk	同學
classroom	fosāt, gaausāt, bāanfóng	課室，教室，班房
clean (n)	gònjehng	乾淨
clean (v)	dásou	打掃
clean and neat	gònjehng kéihléih	乾淨企理
clear, distinct	chingchó	清楚
clear the garbage	dóu laahpsaap	倒垃圾
clever, smart	chùngmìhng	聰明
clever and smart	chùngmìhng lìhngleih	聰明伶俐
climb	pàh	爬
clinic	chánliuhsó, yīlìuhsó	診療所，醫療所
clock, bell	jūng	鐘
close (book, eye, box, etc.)	hahpmàaih	合埋
close (door, window)	sāan	閂
close (in relationship)	mahtchit	密切
closely related	chàn	親

20

closing time (for business)	sàusíh	收市
cloth, material	bou	布
clothes, dress	sāam	衫
clothing	yìfuhk	衣服
cloud	wàhn	雲
club	kēuilohkbouh	俱樂部
clumsy, awkward	leuhngjeuhn	論盡
coach, instructor	gaaulihn	教練
coal	mùih	煤
coat	lāu	褸
Coca Cola	(hóháu) hólohk	（可口）可樂
cock	gāigūng	鷄公
cockroach	gaahkjáat	甲由
cocktail party	gāiméihjáuwúi	鷄尾酒會
coffee	gafē	咖啡
coffin	gùnchòih	棺材
coincidental	kíu	〔嚙〕
cold	dung	凍
cold (usually for weather)	láahng	冷
cold cream	syutfāgōu	雪花膏
cold dish	láahngpún	冷盤
cold meat	dungyuhk	凍肉
collar	léhng	領
collar pin	léhng jām	領針
colleague	tùhngsih	同事
colour	ngàahnsìk	顏色
colour picture	chóisìkséung	彩色相
colour-blindness	sìkmàahng	色盲
colourful, gaudy	nǵhngàahnluhksìk	五顏六色
coma	yàuhāak	休克
comb hair	sòtàuh	梳頭
comb, to comb	sò	梳
come	làih	嚟
come back	fāanlàih	番嚟
come in	yahplàih	入嚟

21

come up	séuhnglàih	上嚟
comfortable	syùfuhk	舒服
comical, funny	waahtkài	滑稽
comics (book or magazine)	maahnwá, gùngjáisyù	漫畫，公仔書
commerce	sèungyihp	商業
commercial port	sèungfauh	商埠
commission, brokerage	yúnggām	佣金
commit suicide	jihsaat	自殺
common	póutùng	普通
common saying	juhkwá, juhkyúh	俗話，俗語
common sense	sèuhngsīk	常識
communism	guhngcháanjyúyih	共產主義
communist party	guhngcháandóng	共產黨
company, corporation	gùngsì	公司
compare	béigaau	比較
compassionate	m̀yánsàm	唔忍心
compel, supervise	gàamjyuh	監住
compensate, compensation	pùihsèuhng	賠償
compete	dau	鬥
competition	béichoi	比賽
complete	chàihbeih	齊備
completely, 100%, extremely	sahpfān	十分
complicated	fūkjaahp	複雜
compose	jok, sé	作，寫
composer	jokkūkgā	作曲家
compulsorily	gaapngáang	夾硬
computer	dihnnóuh	電腦
conceivable, deduce	hó-séung-yìh-jì	可想而知
concept	gùnlihm	觀念
concern	gwàansàm, gwajyuh	關心，掛住
concert	yàmngohkwúi	音樂會

concubine	chipsih	妾侍
concur, agree	jaansihng	贊成
condition (of a patient)	behngchihng	病情
conductor, to conduct	jífāi	指揮
confections, refreshment	dímsām	點心
conference	wuihyíh	會議
conflicts	chùngdaht	衝突
Confucianist, Confucianism	Húnggaau	孔教
Confucius	Húngjí	孔子
congee, rice gruel	jūk	粥
congenital	tìnsàang	天生
congratulate, congratulations	gùnghéi	恭喜
connect	lìhnjip	連接
connect (a telephone etc.)	bok, jip	駁，接
connection, relevance	gwàanhaih	關係
conscience	lèuhngsàm	良心
conservative	bóusáu	保守
consider, think it over	háauleuih	考慮
consider with dislike	yìhm	嫌
console, comfort	ngònwai	安慰
constipation	bihnbei	便秘
constitution	hinfaat	憲法
construct	ginjūk, héi	建築，起
construction company	ginjūk gùngsi	建築公司
construction work	gùngchìhng	工程
consul	lihngsi	領事

consul general	júnglíhngsí	總領事
consulate	líhngsigún	領事館
consulate general	júnglíhngsígún	總領事館
consult a dictionary	chàh jihdín	查字典
consult with, discuss	sèunglèuhng	商量
consultant, advisor	gumahn	顧問
contact	jipjūk	接觸
contact lenses	yányìhng ngáahngéng	隱形眼鏡
contagious disease	chyùhnyíhmbehng	傳染病
container (for goods)	fogwaih	貨柜
contemplate, think	nám/lám	恁
contented	jijūk, ngònlohk	知足，安樂
contents, list	muhkluhk	目錄
contest, compete, competition	béichoi	比賽
continuously	gaijuhk	繼續
contract	hahpyeuk, hahptùhng	合約，合同
contractor (of a building project)	sìhngginsēung	承建商
contradictory, contradiction	màauhtéuhn	矛盾
contrary to expectations	gēuiyín, gēuiyìhn	居然
contribute, contribution	gunghin	貢獻
control	hungjai	控制
convenient	fòngbihn	方便
convolvulus	hìnngàuhfā	牽牛花
cook (n)	chyùhsī, jyúfáhn	廚師，煮飯
cook (v)	jyú, jyúfaahn	煮，煮飯

cooked rice	faahn	飯
cooked, ripe	suhk	熟
cookies, crackers	bénggōn	餅乾
cool	lèuhng, lèuhngsóng	涼、涼爽
cooperate, cooperative	hahpjok	合作
cooperatively (coll.)	gaapsáu-gaapgeuk	夾手夾脚
cope with, handle	yingfuh	應付
copper, bronze	tùhng	銅
copy (v)	chàau	抄
coral	sàanwùh	珊瑚
corn	sūkmáih	粟米
corn oil	sūkmáihyàuh	粟米油
corn soup	sūkmáihgāng	粟米羹
corner	goklōktáu	角落頭
corporate business	gúfán sāangyi	股份生意
correct (an error)	gói	改
correct, fit	ngāam	啱
corrupt	fuhbaaih	腐敗
corsage	kàmtàuhfā	襟頭花
cosmetics	fajōngbán	化裝品
cost of living	sàngwuht siufai	生活消費
cotton	mìhnfā	棉花
cough	kāt, kātsau	咳，咳嗽
count	gai	計
counter	gwaihmín	柜面
countless	sóubātjeuhn	數不盡
country	gwokgā	國家
couple, husband and wife	lèuhngfūchài, lèuhngfūfúh, lèuhnggùngpó	兩夫妻，兩夫婦，兩公婆
courage	yúhnghei	勇氣

course, curriculum	fochìhng	課程
courtsy	láihmaauh	禮貌
cover (v)	kám	冚
cover, lid	goi	蓋
crab	háaih	蟹
cramp	chàugàn	抽筋
crane	hohk, hók	鶴
crash into, hit	pung	碰
crazy	sàhn gìng, chìsin	神經，黐綫
cream	geihlìm	忌廉
credit	seunyuhng	信用
credit card	seunyuhngkāat	信用咭
cremate	fójong	火葬
cricket	sīksēut	蟋蟀
crime	jeuih	罪
crispy	cheui	脆
criticize, criticism	pàipìhng	批評
crocodile	ngohkyùh	鱷魚
cross (n)	sahpjihgá	十字架
cross over	gwo	過
cross-harbour tunnel	hóidái seuihdouh	海底隧道
crow	wūngā	烏鴉
crowded	bīk	逼
cruet-stand	ńghmeihgá	五味架
crutch	gwáaijéung	拐杖
cry, weep	haam	喊
cucumber	chènggwà	青瓜
cufflinks	jauhháunáu	袖口鈕
cultivate, (give care to younger generation)	jòipùih	栽培
culture	màhnfa	文化
cultured, well-behaved	sìmàhn	斯文

cultured pearl	yéuhngjyū	養珠
cunning	gáauwaaht	狡猾
cup	būi	杯
cupboard in kitchen	chyùhgwaih, wúngwaih	櫥柜，碗柜
cure (v)	yī	醫
curiosity	houkèihsàm	好奇心
curious	houkèih	好奇
currency	fobaih	貨幣
curry	galēi	喀喱
curtain	chēunglim	窗簾
cushion (n)	yíjín	椅墊
cushion (v)	sip	攝
custom	fùngjuhk	風俗
custom-house	hóigwàan	海關
cut (with knife)	chit	切
cut (with scissors)	jín	剪
cut apart	chithòi	切開
cute	dākyi, cheuiji	得意，趣緻
cypress	paak	柏

D

daddy	bàhbā	爸爸
daffodil	séuisìnfā	水仙花
dail the wrong number	daapchosin, dácho	搭錯線，打錯
daily	yahtsèuhng, múihyaht	日常，每日
daily life	sāngwuht	生活
daisy	chōgùk	雛菊
dance	tiumóuh	跳舞
dancing party	móuhwúi	舞會
dandelion	pòuhgùngyìng	蒲公英
dangerous, danger	ngàihhím	危險
dare	gám	敢

daring, foolhardy	daaihdáam	大膽
dark, black	hāak	黑
dark color	sāmsīk	深色
dark green	sāmluhk (sīk)	深綠（色）
data	jīlíu	資料
date	yahtkèih	日期
date of birth	chēutsāng yahtkèih	出生日期
daughter	néui	女
dawn	tìnmūnggwòng	天濛光
day, date	yaht	日
day after tomorrow	hauhyaht	後日
day before yesterday	chìhnyaht	前日
day of the month	houh	號
daytime	yahttáu	日頭
dazzled, blurred	ngáahnfā	眼花
deaf	lùhng	聾
dear, loved	chànngoige	親愛嘅
debate	bihnleuhn	辯論
debt	jaai	債
deceive, cheat	ngāak, tam	呃，諜
December	Sahpyihyuht	十二月
decide, decision	kyutdihng	決定
decorate	jōngsīk	裝飾
deep, dark (of colours)	sàm	深
deep breath	sàmfūkàp	深呼吸
deep fry	ja, jaau	炸
deer	lúk	鹿
definitely	yātdihng	一定
degree (college)	hohkwái	學位
degree, level	chìhngdouh	程度
delay, postpone	yìhnchìh	延遲
delegate, representative	doihbíu	代表
delicious	hóusihk, hóumeihdouh	好食，好味道

delighted, joyful	gòuhing	高興
deliver	sung	送
deliver (letter)	paai	派
demand	yiukàuh	要求
democracy, democratic	màhnjyú	民主
dense, close	maht	密
dentist	ngàhyī	牙醫
dentistry	ngàhfō	牙科
deny	fáuyihng	否認
department (of Univesity)	haih	系
department store	baakfo gùngsī	百貨公司
depend upon	yíkaau, kaau	倚靠，靠
depends on	tái	睇
deposits, savings	chyùhnfún	存款
deserted (area)	pīnpik	偏僻
design	chitgai	設計
designer	chitgaisī	設計師
desk	syùtói	書枱
dessert	tìhmbán	甜品
destine	jíng dihng	整定
destiny	mihngwahn	命運
destroy	powaaih	破壞
detective	jingtaam	偵探
detergent	sáigitjīng	洗潔精
determinately, determination	kyutsām	決心
develop, expand	faatjín	發展
devil, Satan	mōgwái	魔鬼
devoted, very patient	hóu sāmgèi	好心機
diagnose	táijing, chánjing	睇症，診症
diagonally opposite	chèhdeuimihn	斜對面
dialects	fòngyìhn	方言
diamond	jyunsehk	鑽石

diarrhoea	tóuhngò, tóuhse	肚疴，肚瀉
diary	yahtgei	日記
dictionay	jihdín	字典
did not expect	gúmdou	估唔到
die, dead	séi	死
died (of sick-ness)	behngséi	病死
difference	fànbiht	分別
difficult	nàahn	難
difficulty	kwannàahn	困難
dig	gwaht	掘
digestion, digest	siufa	消化
dignified, generous	daaihfōng	大方
dim, dark	ngam	暗
dime	hòuhjí	毫子
dining room (at home)	faahntēng	飯廳
dining table	chāantói	餐枱
dinner	máahnfaahn, máahnchāan	晚飯，晚餐
dinner knife	chāandōu	餐刀
dinner party	chāanwúi	餐會
dip into	dim	點
diplomacy	ngoihgāau	外交
diplomat	ngoihgāaugùn	外交官
directly	jihkjip	直接
director, head of a section	jyúyahm	主任
dirty	wūjòu	污糟
disappointed	sātmohng	失望
disco	diksihgōu	的士高
discriminate, discrimination	kèihsih	歧視
discuss (in order to solve a pro-blem)	tóuleuhn	討論

disease	jahtbehng	疾病
dish of food	sung	餸
dish-washer	sáiwúngèi	洗碗機
dissimilar, different	m̀tùhng	唔同
distinguish	fāndākchēut	分得出
distress, suffering	tungfú	痛苦
disturb, trouble	sòuyíu	騷擾
divide into	fànsèhng	分成
divorce	lèihfān	離婚
do	jouh	做
do as one wishes	jihbin	自便
do business	jouhsāangyi	做生意
do homework	jouh gùngfo	做功課
do not (imperative)	m̀hóu	唔好
do one's best	jeuhnlihk	盡力
dock, park	paak	泊
doctor	yīsāng	醫生
doctor of surgery, surgeon	ngoihfō yīsāng	外科醫生
doctor's fee	chán gàm	診金
doctor's private office	yīmouhsó	醫務所
doctrine, -ism	jyúyih	主義
document	màhngin	文件
dog	gáu	狗
doll	gùngjái, yèuhngwāwā	公仔，洋娃娃
dollar	mān, ngàhnchin	蚊，銀錢
donate	gyūn	捐
donate money	gyùnchin	捐錢
donation	gyùnfún	捐款
door, entrance	mùhnháu	門口
door, gate	mùhn	門
door bell	mùhnjùng	門鐘
door keeper	hōngāang	看更

31

door key	mùhnsih	門匙
dormitory	sūkse, sūkséh	宿舍
double	gāpúih	加倍
double registered	sèunggwahouh	雙掛號
double room	sèungyàhnfóng	雙人房
doubt (v)	wàaihyìh	懷疑
down cast	móuh sāmgèi	冇心機
downstairs, the ground floor	làuhhah	樓下
drag	tō	拖
dragon	lùhng	龍
drain (for clean water)	séuikèuih	水渠
draw (as blood)	chàu	抽
draw, paint	waahk	畫
dream	muhng	夢
dream of	muhnggin	夢見
dress (n)	sāam	衫
dress (v)	jeuk	着
dress, adorn	dábaan	打扮
drink	yám	飲
drinking-fountain	yámyuhngpanchyùhn	飲用噴泉
drinking straw	yámtúng	飲筒
drive (a car)	jāchè	揸車
driver	sigèi	司機
driving license, license plate	chèpàaih	車牌
drop off, fall off	latjó	甩咗
drug store	yeuhkfòhng	藥房
drugs	duhkbán	毒品
drum	gú	鼓
drunk, tipsy	yámjeui	飲醉
dry	gōn	乾
dry-cleaning	gōnsái	乾洗
duck	ngaap	鴨

due to, because of..reason	yànwaih . . . ge gwàanhaih	因爲……嘅關係
dull, bored	muhn	悶
durable, (lasting)	kàmsái, kàm	抌使，抌
dust (n)	chàhn	塵
dynasty	chìuh, chìuhdoih	朝，朝代

E

each other	béichí, béichígàan	彼此，彼此間
eager	hóuséung	好想
eagle	yìng	鷹
ear	yíh, yíhjái	耳，耳仔
ear-nose-throat department	yíh-beih-hàuhfō	耳鼻喉科
ear-rings	yíhwáan	耳環
early	jóu	早
earn	jaahn	賺
earnest	yihngjàn	認眞
earth, globe	deihkàuh	地球
east	dùng	東
Easter	Fuhkwuhtjit	復活節
easy	yih, yùhngyih	易，容易
eat	sihk	食
eat at teahouse, drink tea	yámchàh	飲茶
eclipse (of the moon)	yuhtsihk	月蝕
eclipse (of the sun)	yahtsihk	日蝕
economy, economics	gìngjai	經濟
edit, editor	pīnchāp	編輯
editor-in-chief	júngpīnchāp	總編輯
editorial	séhleuhn	社論

educate, education	gaauyuhk	教育
eel	síhn	鱔
efficient	yáuhhaauhléut	有效率
effort	nóuhlihk	努力
egg	dáan	蛋
egg-beater	dádáangēi	打蛋機
egg white	dáanbaahk	蛋白
egg yolk	dáanwóng	蛋黃
eight	baat	八
elbow	sáujāang, jáau	手踭，肘
elder brother	agō	阿哥
elder sister	gājē	家姊
elect	syún	選
election, elect	syúngéui	選舉
electric fan	fùngsin	風扇
electric iron	dihntongdáu	電熨斗
electric light	dihndāng	電燈
electric plug	chapsōu	插蘇
electric rice cooker	dihnfaahnbōu	電飯煲
electric stove	dihnlòuh	電爐
electrical appliance	dihnhei	電器
electricity	dihn	電
electricity bill	dihnfai	電費
elegant	gòugwai, simàhn	高貴，斯文
elephant	(daaihbahn) jeuhng	（大笨）象
elevator, lift	singgonggēi, līp	升降機，□
eliminate	siumiht	消滅
embarrassed, ashamed to	m̀hóuyisi	唔好意思
embassy	daaihsigún	大使館
embrace, hug	láamjyuh	攬住
embroidered, embroidering	saufā	綉花
emergency	gángāpsihgín	緊急事件

emergency room in hospital	gāpjingsāt	急症室
emperor	wòhngdai	皇帝
emphasize	jyujuhng, kéuhngdiuh	注重，强調
employer	sihtáu	事頭
empty	hùngge	空嘅
encourage	gúlaih	鼓勵
encourage by means of reward	jéunglaih	獎勵
encyclopedia	baakfōchyùhnsyù	百科全書
end (v)	gitchūk	結束
end of street	gāaiháu, gāaiméih	街口，街尾
end of the month	yuhtdái, yuhtméih	月底，月尾
end of the year	nìhndái, nìhnméih	年底，年尾
endure, suffer	ngàaih	捱
enemy	dihkyàhn	敵人
engagement (promise to marry)	dihngfān	訂婚
engineer	gùngchìhngsī	工程師
England	Yìnggwok	英國
English (language)	Yìngmàhn, Yìngmán	英文
enjoy, appreciate	yànséung	欣賞
enjoy, enjoyment	héungsauh	享受
enlarge	fongdaaih	放大
enough	gau	夠
entertain	jiudoih	招待
enthusiastic	lohklihk, yihtsām	落力，熱心
entirely, completely	yùhnchyùhn	完全
entrance	yahpháu	入口
entrust, request	tok, baaitok	託，拜託
envelope	seunfùng	信封
environment	wàahnging	環境
envy (v)	sihnmouh, douhgeih	羨慕，妒忌

35

epidemic disease	làuhhàhngjing	流行症
equal to	dángyù	等於
equality, equal	pìhngdáng	平等
equipment	chitbeih	設備
eraser (rubber)	chaatjígàau	擦紙膠
error, mistake	cho	錯
escalator	dihntài	電梯
escort, see off	sung	送
especially	yàuhkèihsih	尤其是
establish, set up	ginlahp	建立
established by government or community	gùnglahp	公立
Europe	Ngāujàu	歐洲
even	lìhn . . . dōu	連……都
even, even to the extent of	sahmji	甚至
even if . . .	jīksí . . . dōu	即使……都
even number	sēungsou	雙數
evening, night-time	yehmáahn, yehmáahnhāak	夜晚，夜晚黑
evening dress	máahnláihfuhk	晚禮服
evening party	máahnwúi	晚會
ever since	jihchùhng	自從
every	múih	每
everywhere	dousyu, syusyu	到處，處處
evidence	jinggeui	證據
evil	jeuihngok	罪惡
exaggerate	kwàjèung	誇張
examination paper	sihgyún	試卷
examine	gímchàh	檢查
examine, take an examination	háausíh	考試
examining room	chánjingsāt	診症室
example	laih, laihjí	例，例子
example, model	bóngyeuhng	榜樣
exceedingly, very	gwáigam	鬼咁

excellent	hóudougihk	好到極
exchange, interchange	gàauwuhn	交換
exchange rate	wuihléut	滙率
excited, tense	gánjèung	緊張
exercise	lihnjaahp	練習
exercise book	lihnjaahpbóu	練習簿
exert one's strength	chēutlihk	出力
exhausting	sokhei	索氣
exhibit, display	jínláahm	展覽
exhibition	jínláahmwúi	展覽會
exit	chēutháu	出口
expand	kwongchùng	擴充
expand, swell	pàahngjeung	膨脹
expected date of delivery	yuhcháankèih	預產期
expenses	faiyuhng	費用
expensive	gwai	貴
experience (n)	gingyihm	經驗
experience (v)	táiyihm, gámsauh	體驗，感受
expert	jyūngā	專家
explain, interpret	gáaisīk, gáai	解釋，解
explode	baau	爆
export	(wahn)chēutháu	（運）出口
export commodity	chēutháufo	出口貨
express, signify	bíusih	表示
expression (of emotion)	bíuchìhng	表情
exquisite	gwātjí	骨子
extension (telephone)	noihsin	內線
extra	ngaahkngoih	額外
extra large	gādaaihmáh	加大碼
extraordinarily, exceptionally	fèisèuhng	非常

extravagent	chèchí	奢侈
extremely	m̀jìgéi, bātjìgéi	唔知幾,不知幾
eye	ngáahn	眼
eye drops	ngáahnyeuhkséui	眼藥水
eye shadow	ngáahnkoigōu	眼蓋膏
eyebrow	ngáahnmèih	眼眉
eyebrow pencil	meihbāt	眉筆
eyelashes	ngáahnjihtmòuh	眼睫毛

F

fable	yuhyìhn	寓言
face	mihn	面
face, confront	mihndeui	面對
face, look on	heung	向
face to face	dòngmín	當面
facilitate	leihbihn	利便
facilities, fixture	chitbeih	設備
fact	sihsaht	事實
factory	gùngchóng, chóng	工廠,廠
fail, failure	sātbaaih	失敗
faint, dizzy	wàhn, tàuhwàhn	暈,頭暈
fair, just	gùngpìhng	公平
fairly, rather	géi	幾
fairy	sàhnsìn	神仙
faith	seunsàm	信心
fall	dit	跌
fall, autumn	chāutìn	秋天
fall down	daatdài	嚹低
fall down on ...	ditlohk ...	跌落
false teeth	gángàh	假牙
false, untrue	gá	假
familiar with	suhk	熟
family	gàtìhng	家庭
family clan	gàjuhk	家族

family members	gāyàhn	家人
famous, well-known	chēutméng	出名
fan (n)	sin	扇
fan (v)	put	撥
far	yúhn	遠
Far East	yúhndùng	遠東
farewell party	fùnsungwúi	歡送會
farm	nùhngchèuhng	農場
farmer	nùhngfù	農夫
farsighted, hyperopia	yúhnsih	遠視
fashionable	sìhmōu	時髦
fashions	sìhjòng	時裝
fast, quick	faai, faaicheui	快，快趣
fat & short	fèihfèihngáingái	肥肥矮矮
fat, obese	fèih	肥
fate	mihngwahn	命運
father	bàhbā	爸爸
father (not used in direct address)	fuhchàn	父親
father (slang)	lóuhdauh	老豆
Father's Day	fuhchàn jit	父親節
fatherland	jóugwok	祖國
fear, be afraid of	pa	怕
fearful	hópa	可怕
February	yihyuht	二月
fee	fai	費
feed	wai	餵
feel, sense	gokdāk	覺得
feel in pocket or bag	ngàhm	唸
feel with one's hand	mó, mō	摸
feelings, mood	sàmchìhng	心情

ferryboat	gwohóisyùhn	過海船
festival	jit, jityaht	節,節日
fetch, get	ló	攞
few, little	síu	少
fiance	meihfānfù	未婚夫
fiancee	meihfānchài	未婚妻
fiction, novel	síusyut	小說
field, farmland	tìhn	田
fight	dágàau	打交
fight for	jàang	爭
fight the fire	gaufó	救火
figure up a bill (usually used in a restaurant)	màaihdāan	埋單
filial	haauseuhn	孝順
fill, stuff	sāk	塞
fill in a form	tìhnbíu	填表
film	fēilám	菲林
finally	jēutjì	卒之
find	wán	搵
find out, discover	faatyihn	發現
fine (money paid as punishment)	fahtfún	罰款
fine (of weather)	chìhnglóhng	晴朗
fine, minute	yausai	幼細
finger	sáují	手指
finger-nail	jígaap	指甲
finger-print	jímòuh, jímàhn	指模,指紋
finish	yùhn	完
fire	fó	火
fire-cracker	paaujéung	炮仗
fire-engine	siufòhngchè, fójūkchè	消防車,火燭車
fire-escapes	wàhntài	雲梯
fire-place	bīklòuh	壁爐
firewood	chàaih	柴

fireworks	yīnfā	烟花
firm, safe	wánjahn	穩陣
first	daihyāt	第一
first class	tàuhdáng	頭等
first prize	tàuhjéung	頭獎
fish	yú	魚
fish, fishing	diuyú	釣魚
five	ńgh	五
fix, arrange	gáaudihm	攪掂
fixed deposit	dihngkèih chyùhnfún	定期存款
flashlight	dihntúng	電筒
flashlight (of the camera)	símgwòngdàng	閃光燈
flat, level	pìhng	平
flat tyre	baautāai	爆呔
flatter	gùngwàih	恭維
flavor, taste	meihdouh	味道
flea	sāt	虱
flee, escape	jáunaahn	走難
flimsy, feeble	fahohk	化學
float	fàuh	浮
floating restaurant	hóisīnfóng	海鮮舫
floor	deihhá, deihbáan	地下，地板
floors (in a building)	chàhng	層
flour	mihnfán	麵粉
flourishing, prosperous	wohng	旺
flower	fā	花
flower garden	fāyún	花園
flower market	fāsíh	花市
flower-pot	fāpùhn	花盆
fly (n)	wūyīng	烏蠅
fly (v)	fēi	飛
fly-over, over-pass	tinkiuh	天橋

41

flying time	fèihàhng sìhgaan	飛行時間
fog, mist	mouh	霧
folding umbrella	sūkgwàtjē	縮骨遮
folk song	màhngō	民歌
follow	gàn(jyuh)	跟（住）
food	sihkmaht	食物
fool (n)	chéunchòih	蠢材
foolish, stupid	sòh	傻
foot (measure)	chek	尺
foot (part of the body)	geuk	腳
foot brake	geukjai	腳掣
foot-bridge	hàahngyàhn tìnkìuh	行人天橋
for, for the sake of	waih	為
for example	laihyùh, peiyùh	例如，譬如
for instance, if supposing	peiyùh, peiyùhwah	譬如，譬如話
for rent, to let	chēutjòu	出租
force, compel	bīk	迫
force, supervise	gāam(jyuh)	監（住）
forceps	kím	鉗
forehead	ngaahktàuh	額頭
foreign country	ngoihgwok	外國
foreigner	(fàan)gwáilóu, ngoihgwokyàhn	（番）鬼佬，外國人
forest	sàmlàhm	森林
forget	m̀geidāk	唔記得
forgive, excuse	yùhnleuhng	原諒
fork	chā	叉
form (for information)	bíu	表
formal, offical	jingsīk	正式
formal dinner, banquet	jáujihk, yinwuih	酒席，宴會
formal dress	láihfuhk	禮服
formal visit	baaifóng	拜訪

42

formerly, previously	yìhchìhn, gauhsìh	以前，舊時
fortunate, lucky	hóuchói	好彩
forward (a letter)	jyún	轉
found	ginlahp, chitlahp	建立，設立
foundation	gèichó	基礎
foundation-fund	gèigàm	基金
fountain	panséuichìh, panchyùhn	噴水池，噴泉
fountain pen	mahkséuibāt	墨水筆
four	sei	四
fox	wùhléi	狐狸
fragrant	hèung	香
France	Faatgwok	法國
frank, frankly	táanbaahk	坦白
frank, outspoken	sēutjihk	率直
free (not busy)	dākhàahn	得閑
free of charge	míhnfai	免費
freedom, free	jihyàuh	自由
freezer	bīnggaak	冰格
freighter	fosyùhn	貨船
French (language)	Faatmàhn	法文
fresh	sānsìn	新鮮
fresh water	táahmséui	淡水
Friday	láihbaaingh	禮拜五
fried noodles	cháaumihn	炒麵
fried rice	cháaufaahn	炒飯
friend	pàhngyáuh	朋友
friendly	yáuhsihn	友善
friendship	yáuhyìh, yáuhngoi	友誼，友愛
frighten	haak	嚇
frightened	haakchàn	嚇親
frog	chìngwà	青蛙
from	hái	喺
from afar	lèihyúhn	離遠
from now on	chùhnggāmyíhhauh	從今以後

from time to time	gáumgáu, noihbātnói	久唔久， 耐不耐
front	chìhnbihn	前便
front door	chìhnmún	前門
frown	jaumèihtàuh	皺眉頭
frozen food	gāpdungsihkmaht	急凍食物
fruit	sāanggwó	生果
fruit juice	gwójāp	果汁
fry	jin	煎
fry (stir)	cháau	炒
frying-pan	pihngdáiwohk	平底鑊
fulfill one's duty	jeuhn jaakyahm	盡責任
full (stomach)	báau	飽
full, filled	múhn	滿
full house	✓múhnjoh	滿座
full name	singmihng	姓名
full of life, active	sāangmáahng	生猛
fund	gìngfai	經費
funeral	sōngláih	喪禮
funeral home	banyìhgún	殯儀館
funny, ridiculous	hóusiu	好笑
fur	pèihchóu	皮草
furlough	yàuga	休假
furniture	gāsī	傢俬
furthermore, moreover	yìhché	而且
future	jèunglòih	將來
future prospect	chìhntòuh	前途

G

gab	ngāp	噏
gall stone	dáamsehk	膽石
gamble	dóuchín	賭錢

gambler	laahndóugwái, dóutòuh	爛賭鬼，賭徒
game, recreation	yàuhhei	游戲
garbage	laahpsaap	垃圾
garbage can	laahpsaaptúng	垃圾桶
garden	fāyún	花園
gardener	fāwòhng	花王
gasoline	dihnyàuh	電油
gasoline station	yàuhjaahm	油站
gather up (things)	jāpmàaih	執埋
general, common	póupin, póutùng	普遍，普通
general condition of ...	daaihjige chìhngyìhng	大致嘅情形
general idea	daaihjige yisi	大致嘅意思
general manager	júnggingléih	總經理
generator	faatdihngēi	發電機
generous	futlóu, hóngkoi	闊佬，慷慨
gentleman	sānsí	紳士
geography	deihléih	地理
German (language)	Dākmàhn	德文
Germany	Dākgwok	德國
get, fetch	ló	攞
get, receive	sàudóu, dākdou	收到，得到
get along	sèungchyú	相處
get off (a train, bus, etc.)	lohkchè	落車
get on (a train or bus, etc.)	séuhngchè	上車
get on a boat	séuhngsyùhn	上船
get on a plane	séuhngfēigèi, séuhnggèi	上飛機，上機
get out	chēutheui	出去
get up	héisàn	起身
ghost, devil	gwái	鬼
gift, present	láihmaht	禮物
ginger	gēung	薑

girl	néuihjái	女仔
give	béi	俾
give (a present)	sung	送
give (disease to someone else)	chyùhnyihm	傳染
give a name	héiméng, góiméng	起名，改名
give a party	chénghaak	請客
give a speech	yíngóng	演講
give an example	géuilaih	舉例
give birth	sāang	生
give New Year's greetings	baainìhn	拜年
glad to, a pleasure to	lohkyi	樂意
glass	bōlēi	玻璃
glass for drinks	bōlèibui, séuibui	玻璃杯，水杯
glasses (optical)	ngáahngéng	眼鏡
gleam, flash	sim	閃
globe	deihkàuhyìh	地球儀
gloves	sáumaht, sáutou	手襪，手套
glue	gàauséui	膠水
glue on, stick on	nìhm, tip	黏，貼
glutinous rice	nohmáih	糯米
go	heui	去
go away	ché	扯
go for a honeymoon	douh mahtyuht	渡蜜月
go off from work, get out of work	fonggùng	放工
go out	chēutgāai, chēutheui	出街，出去
go to bed	fangaau	瞓覺
go to class	séuhngtòhng	上堂
go to school	fàanhohk	番學
go to work	fàan gùng	番工
go up	séuhng	上
go upstairs	séuhngláu	上樓
goal, objective	muhkbīu	目標

English	Romanization	Chinese
God	Seuhngdai, Tìnjyú	上帝，天主
god, gods	sàhn	神
going down-hill	lohk che lóu	落斜路
gold	gām	金
gold chain	gāmlín	金鍊
gold color	gāmsīk	金色
goldfish	gāmyú	金魚
golf	gōyihfūkàuh	哥爾夫球
gong	lòh	鑼
good (obedient)	gwàai	乖
good night	jóutáu	早唞
good, well, all right	hóu	好
good-looking	hóuyéung, leng	好樣，靚
goods	fo, fomaht	貨，貨物
gorgeous	gasai	架勢
gossip (n)	sihfēi	是非
gossip (v)	góngsihfēi	講是非
got wet by rain	dahpsāp	搨濕
got, attained	dākdóu	得到
government	jingfú	政府
Governor of Hong Kong	Góngdūk	港督
grab, snatch	chéung	搶
grade, mark	fān (sou)	分（數）
gradually (development)	jihmjím, juhkjím	漸漸，逐漸
graduate	bātyihp	畢業
graduate school	yìhngauyún	研究院
grammar	màhnfaat	文法
grant, endow	chi	賜
granulated sugar	sātòhng	沙糖
grap, hold of	jūkjyuh	捉住
grape	pòuhtàihjí, tàihjí	菩提子，提子
grasp, assurance	bángāak	把握
grasshopper	jamáang	蚱蜢
grateful	gámgīk	感激

47

gravy	jāp	汁
gray (colour)	fūisik	灰色
greasy	yàuhleih	油膩
great (of people)	wáihdaaih	偉大
great, big	daaih	大
greedy	tàamsàm	貪心
green (colour)	luhksīk, luhk	綠色，綠
green wrasse	chèngyi	青衣
grilled pork	chāsiu	叉燒
grind	mòh	磨
groceries	jaahpfo	雜貨
grocery store	jaahpfopóu	雜貨舖
ground floor	deihhá, làuhhah	地下，樓下
ground pepper	wùhjiufán	胡椒粉
group, organization	tyùhntái	團體
grow, plant	jung	種
grow a beard	làuhsōu	留鬚
grow up	jéungdaaih	長大
grumble	ngàhm ngàhm chàhm chàhm	吟吟沉沉
Guangzhou	Gwóngjàu	廣州
guarantee	dāambóu	擔保
guarantor	dāambóuyàhn	擔保人
guess, think	gú	估
guest	yàhnhaak	人客
guest (polite form)	lòihbān	來賓
guide (n)	douhyàuh	導遊
guide (v)	líhngdouh	領導
guitar	gittā	結他
gum	ngàhyuhk	牙肉
gun, rifle, pistol	chēung	槍
gutter (for dirty water)	hāangkèuih	坑渠
gymnasium	táiyuhkgún	體育館

H

habit, custom	jaahpgwaan	習慣
hair (fine)	mòuh	毛
hair (on the head)	tàuhfaat	頭髮
hair style	faatyìhng	髮型
hair stylist	faatyìhngsī	髮型師
haircut (for lady)	jíntàuhfaat	剪頭髮
haircut (for man)	fēifaat	飛髮
hairdresser, barber	léihfaatsī, fēifaatlóu	理髮師，飛髮佬
hairpin	faatgíp, dénggíp	髮夾，頂夾
half	yātbun	一半
hallway, corridor	jáulòhng	走廊
ham	fótéui	火腿
hammer (n)	chéui, chèuihjái	鎚，鎚仔
hammer (v)	dahp	揼
hand	sáu	手
hand bag	sáudói	手袋
hand brake	sáujai	手掣
hand over to	gàaubéi	交俾
hand to, pass	daih	遞
handicraft	sáugùngngaih	手工藝
handkerchief	sáugānjái	手巾仔
handle (a tough problem or person)	deuifuh	對付
handsome	yìngjeun	英俊
handwork	sáugùng	手工
hang	gwa	掛
hang to dry	lohng	晾
hang up	gwahéi	掛起
hanger (for clothes)	yīgá	衣架
happen, occur	faatsāng	發生
happy	hòisàm, fùnhéi	開心，歡喜
happy, happiness	faailohk	快樂

happy birthday	saangyaht faailohk	生日快樂
happy New Year	sànnihn faailohk	新年快樂
hard (quality)	ngaahng	硬
hard, tough	ngàhn	韌
hard-working	kàhnlihk	勤力
hardship, difficulty	gāannàahn	艱難
harm (n)	hoihchyu	害處
harm, injure	sèunghoih	傷害
harmonica	háukàhm	口琴
harmony	wòhhàaih	和諧
harp	syukàhm	豎琴
has a happy look	hóusiuyuhng	好笑容
hat	móu	帽
hate, desire	hahn	恨
have	yáuh	有
have a cold	sèungfùng	傷風
have a dream	faatmùhng	發夢
have a fever	faatsiu	發燒
have a fire	fójūk	火燭
have a holiday	fongga	放假
have a law suit	dá gùnsì	打官司
have a meeting	hòiwúi	開會
have a re-union	tyùhnjeuih	團聚
have a sad look	sàuhyuhng múhnmihn	愁容滿面
have a shock (mentally)	sauh chigīk	受刺激
have a stool	daaihbihn	大便
have good memory	hóugeising	好記性
have indigestion	sihkjaihjó, m̀siufa	食滯咗，唔消化
have not	móuh	冇
have the tooth filled	bóu ngàh	補牙
have to, must	yiu	要
he, she, him, her	kéuih	佢
head	tàuh	頭
head of a team	deuihjéung	隊長

50

head of the family	gājéung	家長
headache	tàuhtung	頭痛
headline	bīutàih	標題
headmaster	haauhjéung	校長
headphones	tèngtúng	聽筒
health	sàntái, gihnhōng	身體，健康
hear	tèng	聽
hearing	ting gok	聽覺
heart disease, heart attack	sàmjohngbehng	心臟病
heart, mind	sàm	心
heart-broken	sèungsàm	傷心
heartbeat	sàmtiu	心跳
heater (for heating water)	yihtséuilòuh	熱水爐
heaven	tìntòhng	天堂
heavy	chúhng	重
heel	geukjāang	脚踭
hell	deihyuhk	地獄
Hello! (on the phone)	wái!	喂
help	bòng, bòngjoh	幫，幫助
help out	gwàanjiu	關照
help! help!	gaumehng a!	救命呀
hemorrhoids	jihchōng	痔瘡
hen	gāiná	鷄姆
hepatitis	gōnyìhm	肝炎
here	nīdouh	呢喥
hereafter, thereafter	yìhhauh	以後
hero	yìnghùhng	英雄
hero (of a play)	jyúgok	主角
heroin	hóilokyìng	海洛英
heroine	néuihjyúgok	女主角
hiccup, hiccough	dásiik	打思噎
hide	nēi, nēimàaih	呢，呢埋

51

high, tall	gòu	高
high heel shoes	gòujàanghàaih	高踭鞋
highway	gùnglouh	公路
hill, mountain	sāan	山
hill-side	sāanbīn	山邊
hinder, stop	jójí	阻止
hire (a person)	chéng	請
history	lihksi	歷史
hit	dá	打
hit the bull's eye	dájung	打中
hobby	sihou	嗜好
hold	jā	揸
hold (in one's arm)	póuh	抱
hold (in one's hand)	nīng jyuh	拎住
hold (meeting, etc.)	géuihàhng	舉行
hole	lūng	窿
holiday	gakèih	假期
home	ngūkkéi	屋企
home for aged people	lóuhyàhnyún	老人院
homeless	mòuh-gā-hó-gwài	無家可歸
homework	gùngfo	功課
honest	lóuhsaht	老實
honey	mahttòhng, fùngmaht	蜜糖，蜂蜜
Hong Kong	Hèunggóng	香港
Hong Kong dollar	Góngjí, Góngngán, Góngbaih	港紙，港銀，港幣
Honolulu	Tàahnhēungsāan	檀香山
honor (n)	wìhngyuh	榮譽
honour with one's presence	séungmín	賞面
hope, expect	hèimohng	希望
horse	máh	馬

horse race	choimáh	賽馬
hospital	yīyún	醫院
hospital fee	jyuhyún fai	住院費
host, master	jyúyán, jyúyàhn	主人
nostess	néuihjyúyán	女主人
hot	yiht	熱
hot sauce	laaht(jiu) jeung	辣（椒）醬
hot spring	wānchyùhn	溫泉
hot tempered	ngok	惡
hot water	yiht séui	熱水
hotel	jáudim	酒店
hour	jùngtàuh	鐘頭
house	ngūk	屋
housemate	tùhngngūk	同屋
how?	dím, dímyéung	點，點樣
how long? (time)	géi nói	幾耐
how many, how much	géidō	幾多
however...	bātgwo ...	不過……
human being	yàhnleuih	人類
human nature	yàhnsing	人性
humble	hìmhèui	懶虛
humorous	yāumahk	幽默
hundred	baak	百
hungry	tóuhngoh	肚餓
hurry up!	faaidī lā!	快啲啦！
hurt, ache	tung	痛
hurt, injure	sauhsēung	受傷
husband	jeuhngfū	丈夫
husband (colloq.)	lóuhgùng	老公
hustling and bustling	yihtnaauh	熱鬧
hut	muhkngūk	木屋
hydrofoil	séuiyihksyùhn	水翼船
hymn, doxology	jaanméihsī, singsī	讚美詩，聖詩
hypnotize	chèuimihn	催眠

I

I, me	ngóh	我
ice	bīng	冰
ice water	bīngséui	冰水
ice-cream	syutgōu	雪糕
ice-cream cone	tihmtúng	甜筒
idea	jyúyi	主意
ideal	léihséung	理想
idiom	sìhngyúh	成語
idle, lazy	láahnsáan	懶散
if, in case	yùhgwó	如果
if only	ji yiu	只要
ignore	fātsih	忽視
ill	behng, m̀syùfuhk	病，唔舒服
illiterate	màhnmàahng	文盲
illness	behng	病
imagination	sàmléih-jokyuhng	心理作用
imagination (creative power)	séungjeuhnglihk	想像力
imitate, imitation	m̀ouhfóng	模仿
immediately, at once	jīkhāak	即刻
immigrant	yìhmàhn	移民
immoral	m̀ouhdouhdāk	冇道德
impatient, be anxious	sàmgàp	心急
imperialism	daigwokjyúyih	帝國主義
import	wahnyahpháu	運入口
import and export	chēutyahpháu	出入口
import commodity	yahphàufo	入口貨
importance	juhngyiusing	重要性
important	juhngyiu	重要

54

impossible	móuhhónàhng, m̀hónàhng	冇可能，唔可能
impression	yanjeuhng	印象
improper	m̀sàam m̀sei ge	唔三唔四嘅
improved	yáuhjeunbouh	有進步
in	hái ...	喺……
in vain	baahkbaahk	白白
in a hurry	chùngmòhng	匆忙
in a low voice	saisēng	細聲
in a moment	yātjahn gāan	一陣間
in a short time	dyúnkèih	短期
in a word	júngjì	總之
in back of	hauhbihn	後便
in case	maahnyāt	萬一
in detail	chèuhngsai	詳細
in detail, carefully	jísai	仔細
in disorder	lyuhn	亂
in fact	sihsahtseuhng	事實上
in front of	chìhnbihn	前便
in general	daaihjiseuhng	大致上
in good spirits	hóujingsàhn	好精神
in order to	waihjó	為咗
in other words	wuhnyìhnjì	換言之
in style	hing	興
in style, stylish	sìhmōu	時髦
in summary	júngjì	總之
in that case	gám	噉
in the middle	jùnggàan	中間
in the past	gwoheui	過去
in the process, carry out	jeunhàhng	進行
in the same boat	tùhng behng sèung lihn	同病相憐
in the world	saigaaiseuhng	世界上
incense stick	hēung	香
inch	chyun	吋

55

incinerator	fàhnfalòuh	焚化爐
include	bāaukwut, bāaumàaih	包括，包埋
income	sàuyahp, yahpsīk	收入，入息
increase	jānggà	增加
indecisive	sàm-daaih-sàm-sai	心大心細
India	Yandouh	印度
indigestable	nàahnsìufa	難消化
indirect, indirectly	gaanjip	間接
individual	goyàhn	個人
industrious, deligent	kàhnlihk	動力
industry	gùngyihp	工業
inexpensive	pèhng	平
inflammation	faatyìhm	發炎
influence, affect	yínghéung	影響
influenza	làuhhàhngsing gám-mouh	流行性感冒
inform, notify	tùngjì	通知
informal	fēijingsīk	非正式
information desk	sēunmahnchyu	詢問處
infulenced by	sauh . . . yínghéung	受……影響
infuriated	fógwán	火滾
inhale	kāp	吸
initiate, launch (a campaign)	faathéi	發起
injection	dájām	打針
ink	mahkséui	墨水
innate, be born with	tìnsàang	天生
inquire	dáting	打聽
inside	léuihbihn, yahpbihn	裡便，入便
inside story	noihmohk	內幕
insist	haih yiu	係要
insistantly	yātméi	一味
insomnia	sātmìhn	失眠

56

inspect, check, examine	gímchàh	檢查
install	jòng, gaau	裝，較
instruct, direct	jísih	指示
instruct, tell	gàaudaai	交帶
instruction, order	fànfu	吩咐
insult	móuhyuhk	侮辱
insurance	yinsō, bóuhím	燕梳，保險
intention	yuhngyi	用意
intentionally	dahkdāng, guyi	特登，故意
interest	hingcheui	興趣
interest (on capital)	leihsīk	利息
interested in	deui . . . yáuh hingcheui	對……有興趣
interesting	yáuhcheui	有趣
interesting, cute	dākyi	得意
interfere, intrude	gònsip	干涉
interior design	sātnoihchitgai	室內設計
intern doctor	sahtjaahp yīsāng	實習醫生
international	gwokjai	國際
international airport	gwokjai gēichèuhng	國際機場
interpreter, translator	chyùhnyihkyùhn, faanyihkyùhn	傳譯員，翻譯員
intersection	sahpjihlouhháu	十字路口
interview	fóngmahn	訪問
interview (for a job)	mihnsíh	面試
intestine	chéung	腸
introduce	gaaisiuh	介紹
invade, invasion	chàmfaahn	侵犯
invent, invention	faatmìhng	發明
investigate	chàh, diuhchàh	查，調查
invitation card	chéngtip, chéngtip	請帖

invite	chéng	請
involve	hìnsip	牽涉
involve others (into trouble)	tòhleuih	拖累
iron	tit	鐵
iron gate	titjaahp	鐵閘
ironing	tongsāam	熨衫
ironing board	tongsāambáan	熨衫板
island	dóu	島
issue, publish	chēut	出
it all depends...	tái . . . làih chau lā!	睇…嚟凑啦！
it doesn't matter	móuhmātsówaih	冇乜所謂
it is a long story	yāt yìhn nàahn jeuhn	一言難盡
it is right	móuh cho	冇錯
it is someone's time to take his turn	lèuhndou . . .	輪到……
it's a deal.	yāt-yìhn-wàih-dihng	一言爲定
Italy	Yidaaihleih	意大利
itchy	hàhn	痕
itinerary	hàhngchìhng(bíu)	行程（表）
ivory	jeuhngngàh	象牙
ivy	chèuhngchēuntàhng	長春籐

J

jacket	ngoihtou	外套
jade	yúk	玉
jail	chóhgāam	坐監
jam	gwójeung	果醬
January	Yātyuht	一月
Japan	Yahtbún	日本
jaw	ngàhgaau	牙較
jazz music	jeuksih yàmngohk	爵士音樂
jealous	douhgeih	妒忌

jeans	ngàuhjáifu	牛仔褲
jerky, trembling	jan	震
Jesus	Yèhsōu	耶穌
jet plane	pansehgēi	噴射機
jetfoil	fèichèuhngsyùhn	飛翔船
jewel, jewelry	sáusīk	首飾
jewelry box	sáusīksēung	首飾箱
job, work	gùngjok	工作
Jockey Club	Máhwúi	馬會
jocky	kèhsì	騎師
jog	páaubouh	跑步
join, take part in	gāyahp	加入
joint	gwāanjit	關節
joke	siuwá	笑話
joke (banter)	góngsíu	講笑
jolt	chok	剒
journey	léuihhàhng	旅行
joy	fùnhéi, faailohk	歡喜，快樂
judge (in a contest)	pìhngpun	評判
judge (in a court)	faatgùn	法官
judge (v)	pundyun	判斷
juice, sauce	jāp	汁
July	Chātyuht	七月
jump	tiu	跳
June	Luhkyuht	六月
junk (ship)	fàahnsyùhn	帆船
jury (in a court)	pùihsámtyùhn	陪審團
just a moment, please	chéng dáng yāt dāng	請等一等
just a moment ago	jingwah, jengwah	正話
just a while ago	tàuhsìn	頭先
just about to	jingjoih yiu	正在要
just at the moment of	jingjoih . . . gójahnsí	正在…… 嗰陣時

just, fair	gùngpìhng	公平
just, only	jihaih	只係
justice	gùngjing	公正

K

keep one's eye on	hāujyuh	吼住
keep, save	làuhfàan	留番
kerosene	fóséui	火水
kettle	chàhbōu	茶煲
key	sósìh	鎖匙
kick	tek	踢
kid	saimānjái	細蚊仔
kidnap	bónggá	綁架
kidney	sáhn, yìu	腎，腰
kill	saat	殺
kilogram	chìnhàk	千克
kilometer	gùngléih	公里
kind, good hearted	hóusàm	好心
kind, merciful	wòhngói, yàhnchìh	和藹，仁慈
kind, sort	júng	種
king	gwokwòhng	國王
kiss (v)	sek	喐
kitchen	chyùhnfóng, chèuih-fóng	廚房
kite	jíyíu	紙鳶
kleenex	jígān	紙巾
knee	sāt (tàuh)	膝（頭）
kneel	gwaih	跪
knife	dōu	刀
knit	jīk	織
knock	hāau	敲
knock on a door	paakmùhn, hāaumùhn	拍門，敲門
know, become acquainted with	sīk	識

know, know about	ji, jidou	知，知道
know how to	sik	識
know something well	suhksik	熟識
knowledge	jisik	知識
Korea	Hòhn'gwok	韓國
Kowloon	Gáulùhng	九龍
Kowloon Tong	Gáulùhngtòhng	九龍塘

L

laboratory	fayihmsāt	化驗室
laboratory technician	fayihmsī	化驗師
laboratory fee	fayihmfai	化驗費
lack of, short of	kyutfaht	缺乏
ladder	tāi	梯
lady	néuihsih	女士
lake	wùh	湖
lamb	yèuhng	羊
lamb chop	yèuhngpá	羊扒
lamp, light	dāng	燈
lampshade	dāngjaau	燈罩
land	deih	地
land (as an airplance)	gonglohk	降落
landlord (owner of house)	ngūkjyú	屋主
landlord (owner of land)	deihjyú	地主
landscape, scenery	fùnggíng	風景
language	yúhyìhn	語言
lantern	dānglùhng	燈籠
large size	daaihmáh	大碼
large, big, older	daaih	大

last night	kàhmmáahn	噚晚
last time	seuhngchi	上次
last week	seuhnggo láihbaai	上個禮拜
last year	gauhnìn, gauhnìhn	舊年
late, later	chìh	遲
late at night	yeh	夜
Latin	Lāaidīngmàhn	拉丁文
laugh, laugh at	siu	笑
launch	yàuhtéhnghó	遊艇河
laundry	sáiyīpóu	洗衣舖
lavatory	chisó	厠所
law	faatleuht	法律
lawn-mower	jínchóugèi	剪草機
lawyer	leuhtsī	律師
lazy	láahn	懶
leader	líhngjauh	領袖
leaf	syuhyihp	樹葉
leafy vegetable	choi	菜
lean (meat)	sau	瘦
lean against	ngàai	挨
lean to one side, be tilted askew	jāk	側
learn, study	hohk	學
learning	hohkmahn	學問
lease	jòuyeuk	租約
leather	pèih	皮
leave, depart	lèihhòi	離開
leave (v)	jáu	走
leave, vacation	gakèih	假期
leave a message	làuhháuseun	留口訊
leave a note	làuhjí, làuhjihtiuh	留紙，留字條
leave hospital	chēutyún	出院
leave work at lunch time	fongngaanjau	放晏晝
left	jó	左
leg	geuk	脚
legal	hahpfaat	合法

legal right	kyùhnleih	權利
legend	chyùhnsyut	傳說
lemon	nìhngmūng	檸檬
lend to	je ... béi	借……俾
lessen, reduce	gáamsíu	減少
lest	míhndāk	免得
let, allow	dáng	等
let loose, put	fong	放
letter	seun	信
letter paper	seunjí	信紙
lettuce	sāangchoi	生菜
level, even, flat	pìhng	平
liberate, liberation	gáaifong	解放
library	tòuhsyùgún	圖書館
library card	jesyùjing	借書證
license (commercial)	pàaihjiu, jāpjiu	牌照，執照
lid, cover	goi	蓋
lie down	fandài	瞓低
life insurance	yàhnsauh yinsō, yàhnsauh bóuhím	人壽燕梳，人壽保險
life-guard	gausāangyùhn	救生員
life-jacket	gausāangyī	救生衣
light	gwòngsin, dānggwòng	光線，燈光
light (not heavy)	hēng	輕
light bulb	dāngdáam	燈胆
light color	chínsik	淺色
light music	hìng yàmngohk	輕音樂
light switch	dāngjai	燈掣
light up	dím	點
lighten (burden, responsibility)	gáamhēng	減輕
lighter	dáfógèi	打火機
lighthouse	dāngtaap	燈塔
lightly (gently)	hehnghēng	輕輕
lightning	símdihn	閃電

lightning-rod	beihlèuihjām	避雷針
like, be fond of	jùngyi	鐘意
like, similar to	chíh	似
lily	baakhahp(fā)	百合（花）
limited	yáuhhaahn	有限
limitless	mòuhhaahn	無限
line	hòhng	行
linguist	yúhyìhnhohkgā	語言學家
linguistics	yúhyìhnhohk	語言學
link	lihnjip	連接
lion	sìji	獅子
lip	(háu)sèuhn	（口）唇
lipstick	seuhngōu	唇膏
liquid	yihktái	液體
list, bill	dāan	單
listen to	tèng	聽
litter-bin	faimahtsēung	廢物箱
little, few	síu	少
live in a school dormitory	geisūk	寄宿
live, stay	jyuh	住
liver	gōn	肝
living room	haaktēng	客廳
living standard	sàngwuht séuijéun	生活水準
lizard	yìhmsé	鹽蛇
loan (money)	jefún	借款
loath to, be reluctant to	m̀sédāk	唔捨得
local	búndeih	本地
located at, in or on	hái	喺
location	deihdím	地點
lock	só	鎖
locomotive	fóchetàuh	火車頭
logical, right	yáuhdouhléih	有道理
London	Lèuhndēun	倫敦
long	chèuhng	長

long (time)	noih	耐
long-distance call	chèuhngtòuh dihnwá	長途電話
long-sleeved	chèuhngjauh	長袖
look, read	tái	睇
look afar	mohng	望
look after, take care of	jiuliuh	照料
look downward	dāpdài (go) tàuh	嗒低（個）頭
look for, call on	wán	揾
look for a job	wángùng	揾工
look like	chíh, hóuchíh	似，好似
look upward	dāamgòu go tàuh	擔高（個）頭
looks familiar	mihnsihn	面善
loose	sùng	鬆
loose, scattered	sáan	散
Lord's prayer	kèihtóumàhn	祈禱文
Los Angeles	Lòhsáang	羅省
lose	m̀ginjó	唔見咗
lose (as a game)	syù	輸
lose (in business)	sihtbún	蝕本
lose (in gambling)	syùchín	輸錢
lose face	diugá	丟架
loss, lose	syúnsāt	損失
lost one's way	dohng sāt louh	蕩失路
lotus	hòhfā	荷花
loud, loudly	daaihsēng	大聲
lovable	hó oi	可愛
love	ngoi, ngoisàm	愛，愛心
love (between opposite sex)	ngoichìhng, nyúnngoi	愛情，戀愛
love-letter	chìhngseun	情信
love story	ngoichìhnggusih	愛情故事
lover	ngoiyàhn, chìhngyàhn	愛人，情人
low	dài	低
low, short	ngái	矮
loyal	jùngsàm	忠心

luck	wahnhei	運氣
lucky	hóuchói	好彩
lucky, happy	hahngwahn, yáuhfūkhei	幸運，有福氣
lucky money (in a red envelope)	laihsih	利是
Lunar calendar	gauhlihk, yàmlihk, nùhnglihk	舊曆，陰曆，農曆
lunch	ngaanjau	晏晝
lung	fai	肺

M

M.A. or M.S.	sehksih	碩士
M.C. (master of ceremony)	siyih	司儀
Macao	Ngoumún, Oumún	澳門
macaroni	tùngsàmfán	通心粉
machine	gèihei	機器
machine-gun	gēigwàanchēung	機關槍
magazine	jaahpji	雜誌
maid servant	néuihgùngyàhn	女工人
mail, send	gei	寄
mailbox (for mailing letter)	yàuhtúng	郵筒
mailbox (for receiving mail)	seunsēung, yàuhsēung	信箱，郵箱
mailman, postman	yàuhchāai	郵差
maintain, support	waihchìh	維持
majority	dòsou, daaihdòsou	多數，大多數
make a date or appointment	yeuk	約
make a draft	héigóu	起稿
make a fortune	faatchòih	發財
make a knot	dálit	打纈
make a living	wánsihk	搵食

make a noise	héung	響
make a phone call	dádihnwá	打電話
make a reserva-tion	dehng	訂
make a turn	jyunwāan	轉彎
make change	jáaujuhk	找贖
make coffee	chùng gafē	冲咖啡
make decision	hah kyutsàm	下決心
make ends meet	jàujyún	周轉
make into	jouhsìhng	做成
make out a list	hōidāan	開單
make profit	jaahn	賺
make public, open	gùnghòi	公開
make tea	chùngchàh	冲茶
make up (in studying)	bóujaahp	補習
make use of	leihyuhng	利用
make war	dájeung	打仗
male	nàahm	男
malodorous, ill smelling	chau	臭
man	nàahmyán	男人
man-made	yàhnjouh	人造
manageable	gàaudākdihm	攪得掂
management, manage	gúnléih	管理
manager	gìngléih	經理
Mandarin	Póutùngwá	普通話
Mandarin duck	yūnyēung	鴛鴦
Mandarin orange	gām	柑
mantis	tòhnglòhng	螳螂
manufacture	jaijouh	製造
manuscript	góu	稿
many	hóudò	好多
map	deihtòuh	地圖
marajuana	daaihmàh	大麻
March	Sàamyuht	三月

market	gāaisíh	街市
marry, get married	gitfān	結婚
mask	mihngeuih	面具
mask (for doctors or nurses)	háujaau	口罩
Mass transit Railway	deihtit	地鐵
master (opp. of apprentice)	sīfú	師傅
mat	jehk	蓆
match (can be compared with)	paakdākjyuh	拍得住
match (fire stick)	fócháai, fóchàaih	火柴
match, competition	béichoi	比賽
match-maker	mùihyán	媒人
material	chòihliu	材料
mathematics	souhohk	數學
matriculation	daaihhohk yuhfō	大學預料
matter, affair	sih	事
May	Ńghyuht	五月
may, might	waahkjé	或者
may not, not necessarily	meihbit	未必
me, I	ngóh	我
meal	faahn	飯
meaning, idea	yisi, yisī	意思
meaningful	yáuhyisī	有意思
measles	màhchán	麻疹
measure	dohk	度
meat	yuhk	肉
medical check-up	gímchàh sàntái	檢查身體
medical fee	yīyeuhk fai	醫藥費
medical insurance	yīyeuhk bóuhím	醫藥保險

medical prescription	yeuhkfōng	藥方
medicine	yeuhk	藥
medicine charge	yeuhkfai	藥費
medium size	jùngmáh	中碼
meet, encounter	yuhdóu	遇到
meet, pick up	jip	接
meet, see	gin	見
meeting, conference	wúi, wuihyíh	會，會議
melody	syùhnléut	旋律
melon, gourd	gwā	瓜
melt	yùhng	溶
member	wúiyùhn	會員
member of a church	gaautòuh, gaauyáuh	教徒，教友
member of a team	deuihyùhn	隊員
members of one's family	chànyàhn	親人
memory	geising	記性
menses, menstruation	yuhtgīng, gìnkèih	月經，經期
mental hospital	sàhn gìng-behngyún	神經病院
mention	góngkahp, tàihkahp	講及，提及
menu (Chinese food)	choipáai	菜牌
menu (Western food)	chāanpáai	餐牌
merits, good points	yāudím	優點
Merry Christmas	sing daan faai lohk	聖誕快樂
messenger	seunchāai	信差
meter	gùngchek	公尺
meter (in a taxi)	māibīu	咪錶
method, way	faatjí, baahnfaat	法子，辦法
Mexico	Mahksāigō	墨西哥
microphone	māi	咪

microwave - oven	mèihbō guhklòuh	微波焗爐
middle school, high school	jùnghohk	中學
midnight	bunyé	半夜
midnight snack	siuyé	宵夜
midwife	johcháansih	助產士
might as well	m̀ngāam	唔啱
mile	māi, léih	咪，哩
military	gwānsih	軍事
military officer	gwāngùn	軍官
milk	ngàuhnáaih	牛奶
milk bottle	náaihjēun	奶樽
milkshake	náaih sīk	奶昔
millionaire	baakmaahnfuyūng	百萬富翁
mind, feel objection to	gaaiyi	介意
mind, intention	sàmyi	心意
mind, pay attention	léih	理
mine	ngóhge	我嘅
minister, pastor	muhksī	牧師
mink fur	diupéi	貂皮
minority	síusou	少數
minute	fàn, fànjùng	分，分鐘
miracle	kèihjīk, sàhnjīk	奇蹟，神蹟
miraculous, incredible	bāthósiyíhge	不可思議嘅
mirror	geng	鏡
miscarry, abort	síucháan	小產
miscellaneous	sāpsāpseuiseui	濕濕碎碎
mischievous, naughty	baakyim, fáandáu	百厭，反斗
miserable, sorrowful	cháam	慘
misjudge	gwaaicho	怪錯
miss, unmarried woman	síujé	小姐

missionary, evangelist	chyùhndouhyàhn, chyùhngaausih	傳道人， 傳教士
misunderstand, misunderstanding	nghwuih	誤會
mix	kàu	溝
mixer	gáaubuhnhei	攪拌器
model	mòuhdahkyìh	模特兒
model, fine example	mòuhfaahn	模範
modern	yihndoih, mōdāng	現代，摩登
modernize, modernization	yihndoihfa	現代化
Monday	láihbaaiyāt	禮拜一
money	chín	錢
money in small denomination	sáanjí, sáanngán	散紙，散銀
monk (Buddist)	wòhséung	和尚
monkey	máhlāu	馬騮
monopoly	jyùnleihkyùhn	專利權
month	yuht	月
monthly ticket	yuhtpiu, yuhtfēi	月票，月飛
mood, atmosphere	heifān	氣氛
moon, moonlight	yuhtgwòng	月光
mooncake	yuhtbéng	月餅
moral	douhdāk	道德
more	dōdī	多啲
more or less	dōsiu	多少
morning	jiutàuhjóu, jiujóu	朝頭早，朝早
morning (forenoon)	seuhngjau	上晝
Moslem, Islamic	Wùihgaau	回教
mosquito	mān	蚊
most	jeui	最
most recently	jeuigahn	最近
mother	màhmā, a mā	媽媽，啊媽
Mother's Day	móuh chàn jit	母親節
motor	mōdá	摩打

71

motorcycle	dihndāanchē	電單車
mouth	háu, jéui	口，嘴
mouthful, puff (of smoke breath, etc.)	daahm	啖
move, arouse	gámduhng	感動
move, change position	yūk	郁
move (things)	bùn	搬
move house	būnngūk	搬屋
movement, campaign	wahnduhng	運動
movie	dihnyíng, hei	電影，戲
Mr., gentleman, teacher, husband (polite)	sinsàang	先生
Mrs., madam, wife (polite), lady (married)	taaitáai	太太
much, many	dò	多
mud	nàih	泥
muddled, follish	wùhtòuh	糊塗
muscle	gēiyuhk	肌肉
muscle cramp	chàugàn	抽筋
museum	bokmahtgún, bokmahtyún	博物館，博物院
music	yàmngohk	音樂
musician	yàmngohkgā	音樂家
mussel	daahmchoi	淡菜
must	yātdihngyiu	一定要
must be, certainly	gánghaih … lā	梗係……啦
mustard paste	gaailaaht	芥辣
mute	ngá	啞
mutton	yèuhngyuhk	羊肉
mutually	wuhsēung	互相
my	ngóhge	我嘅

| myself | ngóhjihgéi | 我自己 |
| mysterious | sàhnbei | 神秘 |

N

nag	lōsò	囉嗦
nail (n, v)	dēng	釘
nail-clippers	jígaapkím	指甲鉗
nail-varnish	jígaapyàuh	指甲油
name	méng	名
name card	kāatpín	卡片
named brand, well known brand	mìhngpàaih	名牌
napkin	chāangān	餐巾
narcissus	séuisīn(fā)	水仙（花）
narrow	jaak	窄
nasal discharge	beih tai	鼻涕
nationality	gwokjihk	國籍
natural science	jihyìhnfōhohk	自然科學
naturalize (as a citizen)	yahpjihk	入籍
naturally	jihyìhn	自然
naughty	yáih, baakyim	曳，百厭
navy	hóigwàn	海軍
near	káhn	近
near, close to	gahnjyuh	近住
neat	kéihléih	企理
neat & tidy	jingchàih	整齊
necessary	bitsēui ge	必須嘅
neck	géng	頸
necklace	génglín	頸鍊
necktie	léhngtāai	領呔
necktie clip	tāaigíp	呔夾
necktie pin	tāaijām	呔針
need, in need of	sèuiyiu	需要
needle	jām	針

negative (attitude)	sìugihk	消極
negative (film)	séungdái	相底
negro	hāakyàhn	黑人
neighbour	lèuhnse	鄰舍
neon sign	gwònggúnjìupàaih, ngàihhùhngdāng	光管招牌, 霓虹燈
nephew	ját	姪
nervous	gánjèung	緊張
nervous breakdown	sàhngingsèuiyeuhk	神經衰弱
never before	chùhnglòihmeih	從來未
new	sàn	新
new style	sànsìk	新式
New Territories	Sàngaai	新界
New Testament	Sànyeuk	新約
New Year's Eve	Chèuihjihk	除夕
New Year's Eve (Chinese New Year)	Nìhnsā'ahmáahn, Daaihchèuihjihk	年卅晚, 大除夕
New York	Náuyeuk	紐約
newly	sàngahn	新近
news	sànmán, sànmàhn	新聞
News agency	tùngseunséh	通訊社
news report	sànmàhn bougou	新聞報告
news script	sànmàhngóu	新聞稿
news, information	sìusìk	消息
newspaper	boují	報紙
Newsstand	boutāan, boujídong	報攤, 報紙檔
next (in position)	gaaklèih	隔籬
next time	hahchi	下次
next year	chēutnín, chēutnìhn	出年
nice	hóu	好
nickname	fāméng	花名
night	yehmáahn	夜晚
night club	yehjúngwúi	夜總會

night-time	máahnhāak, máahntàuhhāak	晚黑，晚頭黑
nightmare	ngokmuhng.	惡夢
nine	gáu	九
no comment	mòuhhófuhnggou	無可奉告
no harm to	bātfòhng	不妨
no matter ..., whether ... or	mòuhleuhn	無論……
no trouble at all	móuh mahntàih gé	冇問題嘅
no wonder	m̀gwaaidāk	唔怪得
no, not	m̀h	唔
no, not any	móuh	冇
nod one's head	ngahptáu	嗌頭
noisy	chòuh	嘈
noontime	ngaanjau	晏晝
normal	jingsèuhng	正常
north	bāk	北
North America	Bākméihjàu	北美洲
northeast	dūngbāk	東北
northwest	sāibāk	西北
nose	beih(gō)	鼻（哥）
not bad	m̀cho	唔錯
not feeling well	m̀haih géi jìngsàhn	唔係幾精神
not interested in	deui ... móuh hingcheui	對……冇興趣
not necessarily	meihbīt	未必
not only	m̀jí	唔止
not until, before	sìnji	先至
note-book	bóu, bātgeibóu	簿，筆記簿
nothing	móuhyéh	冇嘢
notice (n)	tùnggou	通告
notice (v)	jyuyi	注意
notice board	bougou báan	佈告板
noun	mìhnngchìh	名詞
novel	siusyut	小說
November	Sahpyātyuht	十一月

now, at present, at this time	yìhgā	而家
number	houhmáh, houhsou	號碼，號數
nun (Buddist)	sīgù	師姑
nun (Catholic)	sāunéui	修女
nurse	wuhsih, hōnwuh	護士，看護
nursery	tokyìhsó	托兒所
nut	gwóyàhn	果仁
nutrition, nourishment	yìhngyéuhng	營養
nylon stocking	sīmaht	絲襪

O

O dear me! Gosh!	Baihgāfó la	弊傢伙嘞
o'clock, hour	dím, dímjùng	點，點鐘
oatmeal	mahkpín, mahkpèih	麥片，麥皮
obedient	tèngwah	聽話
obey	fuhkchùhng	服從
obligation	yihmouh	義務
observatory	tìnmàhntòih	天文台
observe, observation	gùnchaat	觀察
obstruct, hold up, hinder	jó	阻
obviously	mìhngmìhng	明明
obviously know	mìhng jì	明知
occasion (formal)	chèuhnghahp	場合
occasionally	sìh-bāt-sìh	時不時
occupy	jim	佔
occur, happen	faatsàng	發生
ocean	hóiyèuhng	海洋
October	Sahpyuht	十月
odd number	dāansou	單數
of course	gánghaih, dòngyìhn	梗係，當然
offend	chùngjohng	衝撞

76

offer	tàihgùng	提供
offer money, invest money	chēutchín	出錢
office	baahngūngsāt, séjihlàuh	辦公室，寫字樓
office boy	hauhsāang	後生
officially, formal	jingsīk	正式
officiate at a marriage	jingfān	證婚
officiator at a marriage	jingfān yàhn	證婚人
often, frequently	sìhsìh	時時
oil	yàuh	油
oil pitcher	yàuhjēun	油樽
oil-painting	yàuhwá	油畫
ointment	yeuhkgōu	藥膏
okay!	hóulā!	好喇！
old (aged)	lóuh	老
old (not new)	gauh	舊
old fashioned	gúlóuh	古老
old man	baakyēgūng	伯爺公
old person (polite form)	lóuhyàhngā	老人家
old style	gúlóuh, gauhsīk	古老，舊式
Old Testament	Gauhyeuk	舊約
old woman	baakyēpó	伯爺婆
on (big) sale	daaihgáamga	大減價
on behalf of	doihtai	代替
on day duty	jihkyaht	值日
on every occasion	múihfùhng	每逢
on night duty	jihkyé	值夜
on probation	siyuhng	試用
one	yāt	一
one of...	...jíyāt	之一
one of the best	sóu-yāt-sóu-yih	數一數二
one way	dāanchìhng	單程

onion	yèuhngchùng	洋葱
only, no more than	jihaih . . . jē	只係,⋯⋯啫
only have	jíyáuh	只有
open	dáhòi	打開
open (a book)	kínhòi	揭開
open, unwrap	chaakhòi	折開
open an account in a bank	hòiwuhháu	開戶口
open fire	hòi chèung	開槍
open for business (for the first day)	hòimohk	開幕
operation room	sáuseuhtsāt	手術室
opinion	yigin	意見
opium	baahkfán, ngāpin	白粉,鴉片
opportunity	gèiwuih	機會
oppose, object	fáandeui	反對
opposite (facing)	deuimihn	對面
optimistic	lohkgùn	樂觀
or (as a question)	yīkwaahk	抑或
oral examination	háusíh	口試
orange	cháang	橙
orange (colour)	cháangsīk	橙色
orange juice	cháangjāp	橙汁
orchestra	gúnyìhn ngohkdéui	管弦樂隊
orchid	làahnfā	蘭花
order, command	mihnglihng	命令
order dishes	giusung	叫餸
order merchandise	baahn fo	辦貨
ordinarily	pìhngsìh	平時
ordinary	pìhngsèuhng	平常
ordinary mail	pìhngyàuh, pìhngseun	平郵,平信
ordinary meal	bihnfaahn	便飯
organ	heigùn	器官

organ (musical instrument)	fūngkàhm	風琴
organization	gēigwāan	機關
organize	jóujīk	組織
origin	héiyùhn	起源
originally	búnlòih	本來
orphan	gùyìh	孤兒
orphanage	gùyìhyún	孤兒院
other	kèihtà	其他
other people	yàhndeih	人哋
otherwise	yeuhkm̀haih	若唔係
ought to, should	yìnggòi	應該
ounce	ōnsí	安士
our	ngóhdeihge	我哋嘅
out of order (things)	waaih	壞
outer space	taaihùng	太空
outline	daaihgòng	大綱
outside	chēutbihn, ngoihbihn	出便，外便
outspoken	jihk-chèuhng-jihk-tóuh	直腸直肚
oven	guhklòuh	焗爐
overcoat	daaihl̀au	大褸
overcome	hāakfuhk	克服
overcrowded, congested	bīk	迫
overdo	gwofạhn	過份
overseas Chinese	wàhkiuh	華僑
overslept	fangwolùhng	瞓過龍
overweight	gwochúhng	過重
owe	him	欠
owl	māautàuhyìng	貓頭鷹
owner	jyúyán	主人
oyster	hòuh	蠔

P

pack	jōng	裝
pack luggage	jāphàhngléih	執行李
package, parcel	bāaugwó	包裹
padestrian subway	hàahngyàhn seuihdouh	行人隧道
page	báan, yihp	版，頁
pagoda	taap	塔
painful, sore	tung	痛
paint, put on	yàuh	油
(paint or colour)		
painter	wágā	畫家
pair, couple	deui	對
pajamas, pyjamas	seuihyī	睡衣
palm	sáujéung	手掌
panties	sàamgokfu	三角褲
pants	chèuhngfu	長褲
pantyhose	mahtfu	襪褲
paper	jí	紙
paper bag	jídói	紙袋
paper clip	maahnjihgíp	萬字夾
paradise	tìntòhng	天堂
paragraph	dyuhn	段
paralysis	màhbei, táan	痲痺，癱
pardon, excuse	yùhnleuhng	原諒
parents	fuhmóuh	父母
Paris	Bālàih	巴黎
park (n)	gùngyún	公園
park a car	paakchè	泊車
parking lot	tìhngchèchèuhng	停車場
parking space	chèwái	車位
part, a part of	bouhfahn	部分
participate, join	chāamgā	參加

particular (of good taste or choice)	gónggau	講究
partner	pāatnàh, hahpfóyàhn	拍姆，合夥人
pass, cross	gwo	過
pass a set time	gwojūng	過鐘
pass by	gìnggwo	經過
pass flatus	fong pei	放屁
pass through to	tùngheui	通去
passable, tolerable	gwodākheui, màhmádéi	過得去，麻麻地
passed away, died	gwosàn	過身
passed out, unconscious	bātsíng-yàhnsih	不省人事
passenger	daaphaak	搭客
passport	wuhjiu	護照
paste, thick sauce	jeung	醬
pastime, amusement	sìuhín	消遣
pastry	sāibéng	西餅
pat	paak	拍
patience	noihsing, yánnoihlihk	耐性，忍耐力
patient	behng yàhn	病人
patient (adj)	yánnoih	忍耐
patient's history sheet	behnglihkbíu	病歷表
patriotic	ngoigwok	愛國
patronize	bòngchan	幫趁
pay	béichìn	俾錢
pay (the fee)	gàau	交
pay attention to (person)	chói	睬
pay attention to, take notice of	jyuyi, làuhsàm	注意，留心

pay by instalement	fànkèih fuhfún	分期付款
pay electricity bill	gàau dihnfai	交電費
pay the rent	gàaujòu	交租
pay the tuition	gàau hohkfai	交學費
pay water bill	gàau séuifai	交水費
peace	wòhpìhng	和平
peaceful, quiet	ngònjihng	安靜
peacock	hùngjéuk	孔雀
peak (of hill)	sàandéng	山頂
peanut	fāsāng	花生
pear	léi	梨
pearl	jànjyù	珍珠
Pearl River	Jyūgōng	珠江
peas	chèngdáu	青豆
pediatrics	síuyìhfō	小兒科
pedicab	sàamlèuhnchè	三輪車
peep	jòng	裝
Peking, Beijing	Bākgìng	北京
pen	bāt	筆
pencil	yùhnbāt	鉛筆
pencil sharpener	yùhnbātpáau	鉛筆刨
peninsula	bundóu	半島
pension	yéuhnglóuhgam	養老金
peony	máuhdāan	牡丹
people	yàhnmàhn	人民
peppery, hot	laaht	辣
Pepsi Cola	Baaksihhólohk	百事可樂
perfect	sahp-chyùhn-sahp-méih	十全十美
perform, performance	bíuyín	表演
performer, actor	yínyùhn	演員
perfume	hēungséui	香水
perm	dihnfaat	電髮
permit, grant	pàijéun, jéun	批准，准

persistantly, insist on	ngáanghaih	硬係
personally, in person	chànjih, chànsàn	親自，親身
perspire, sweat	chēuthohn	出汗
pessimistic	bēigùn	悲觀
ph.D.	boksih	博士
pharmaceutical company	yeuhkchóng	藥廠
pharmacist	yeuhkjāisi	藥劑師
Philippines	Fēileuhtbān	菲律賓
philosopher	jithohkgā	哲學家
philosophy	jithohk	哲學
philosophy of life	yàhnsānggùn	人生觀
phoenix	fuhngwòhng, fúng	鳳凰，鳳
phonecall	dihnwá	電話
phonograph record	cheungdíp, cheungpín	唱碟，唱片
photograph (n)	séung	相
photograph (v)	yíngséung	影相
physician, doctor	yīsàng	醫生
physician trained in Chinese medicine	jūngyì	中醫
physician trained in Western medicine	sāiyì	西醫
physics	mahtléih	物理
piano	gongkàhm	鋼琴
pick (fruit or flower)	jaahk	摘
pick up	jāpfàan, jāphéi	執番，執起
pick-pocket	pàhsáu	扒手
picnic	yéhchāan	野餐
picture, painting	tòuhwá, wá	圖畫，畫
pier, dock, wharf	máhtàuh	碼頭
pig	jyū	猪

pile up, pile of	daahp	沓
pill, tablet	yeuhkyún	藥丸
pillow	jámtàuh	枕頭
pillowcase	jámtàuhdói	枕頭袋
pilot (of a plane)	gēijéung	機長
pimple	amchōng	暗瘡
pine	chùhng	松
pink	fánhùhngsīk	粉紅色
pipe	yīndáu	烟斗
piping hot	yihtlaahtlaaht	熱辣辣
pistol	sáuchēung	手槍
pitch dark	hāakmāmā	黑麻麻
pitiful, have pity on	hólìhn	可憐
place, location	deihfòng	地方
plan, plan to	gaiwaahk, dásyun	計劃，打算
plant, cultivate	jung	種
plants	jihkmaht	植物
plastic	sougāau, gāau	塑膠，膠
plastic bag	gāaudói	膠袋
plate	dihp, díp	碟
play	wáan	玩
play a prank	nánfa	撚化
play chess or checker	jūkkéi	捉棋
play hide and seek	jūk nēinēi	捉呢呢
play mahjong	dámàhjeuk	打麻雀
play piano	tàahnkàhm	彈琴
please	m̀gòi	唔該
pleated skirt	baakjipkwàhn	百褶裙
plenty of	daaihbá	大把
pliers	kím	鉗
plum	mùih	梅
ply (use pliers)	kìhm	鉗
pneumonia	fai yìhm	肺炎

pocket	dói	袋
poem, poetry	sī	詩
poet	sīyàhn	詩人
point at	jí	指
point, dot	dím	點
poisoned	jungduhk	中毒
police	gíngchaat, chāaiyàhn	警察，差人
police car	gíngchè	警車
police inspector	bòngbáan	幫辦
police officer	gíngsī	警司
police station	chāaigún, gíngchaatgúk	差館，警察局
policewoman	néuihgíng, chāaipòh	女警，差婆
policy, administrative policy	jingchaak	政策
political party	jingdóng	政黨
political, politics	jingjih	政治
politician	jingjihgā	政治家
pollution	wūyíhm	污染
pomelo, Chinese grape-fruit	lūkyáu, sātìhnyáu	椂柚，沙田柚
poor	kùhng, kùhngfú	窮，窮苦
poor (in quality)	yáih	曳
poor people	kùhng yàhn	窮人
pop singer	làuhhàhng gōsáu	流行歌手
pop song	làuhhàhngkūk	流行曲
population	yàhnháu	人口
pork	jyūyuhk	豬肉
pork chop	jyūpá	豬扒
pork ribs	pàaihgwāt	排骨
pornographic	sīkchìhng, hàahmsāp	色情，鹹濕
position, location	waihji	位置
position, status	deihwaih	地位
positive (attitude)	jīkgihk	積極

85

possible, possibly, possibility	hónàhng	可能
post office	yàuhjinggúk, yàuhgúk	郵政局，郵局
post-secondary college	daaihjyūn	大專
postage	yàuhfai	郵費
postcard	mìhngseunpín	明信片
poster	hóibou	海報
pot	wú, wùh	壺
pot (for cooking)	bōu	煲
potato	syùhjái	薯仔
pound	bohng	磅
pound, ram down	jùng	椿
pour (through a spout)	jàm	斟
pour, pour out	dóu	倒
powder cleaner	heuiwūfán	去污粉
powdered soap	gáanfán	梘粉
power, authority	kyùhnlihk	權力
power, influence	sailihk	勢力
powerful	gaulihk	夠力
practice (in order to learn)	lihnjaahp	練習
praise	jaan, jaanméih	讚，讚美
pray (to God), prayer	kèihtóu, tóugou	祈禱，禱告
preach	chyùhndouh, góngdouh	傳道，講道
precious	bóu gwai	寶貴
precious stones	bóusehk	寶石
preface (of a book)	chìhnyìhn, jeuih	前言，序
pregnant	yáuhsàngéi	有身紀
premier	júngléih	總理
prepare	jéunbeih, yuhbeih	準備，預備
president (of a republic)	júngtúng	總統

Press Office	bougún	報館
press on	gahm	撳
pretend	jadai	詐諦
pretty, handsome	leng	靚
preventive inoculation	yuhfòhngjām	預防針
price	gachìhn	價錢
price of ticket	piuga	票價
priest (Catholic)	sàhnfuh	神父
primary school, grade school	siuhohk	小學
principal, headmaster	haauhjéung	校長
print	yan	印
printed matter	yanchaatbán	印刷品
printing factory	yanchaatchóng	印刷廠
prison	gāamyuhk	監獄
private (owned by oneself)	siyàhn, sigā	私人，私家
privately established	sīlahp, sīlaahp	私立
privileged	wìhnghàhng	榮幸
prize	jéung	奬
probably	daaihkói	大概
procedure, formality	sáujuhk	手續
procelain, chinaware	chìhhei	瓷器
produce	chēut	出
produce, product	chēutcháan	出產
profession, job	jīkyihp	職業
professor	gaausauh	教授
profit	leihyeuhn	利潤
profitable, make profit	jaahnchin	賺錢
program	jitmuhk	節目

progress, improvement	jeunbouh	進步
project (n)	gaiwaahk	計劃
projector	fongyínggèi	放映機
promise (n)	lokyìhn	諾言
promise (v)	yìngsìhng	應承
pronunciation	faatyām	發音
proof, evidence	jinggeui	證據
proof-reader	gaaudeuiyùhn	校對員
property	chòihcháan	財產
prosperous	fàahnwìhng	繁榮
protect, protection	bóuwuh	保護
Protestant, Protestantism	Gēidūkgaau	基督教
proud	gìungouh	驕傲
province	sáang	省
public holiday	gùngjung gakèih	公眾假期
public library	gùngguhng tòuhsyùgún	公共圖書館
public light bus, minibus	sìubā	小巴
public opinion	yùhleuhn	輿論
public relations	gùngguhng gwàanhaih	公共關係
publish	chēutbáan	出版
publisher	chēutbáanyàhn	出版人
pull	māng, lāai	掹，拉
pull open (drawers)	tonghòi	趟開
punish, fine	faht	罰
purge	chìngsyun	清算
purple	jísīk	紫色
purse	ngàhnbāau	銀包
pursue, seek, beg	kàuh	求
push, shove	ngúng, tèui	㩒，推
push aside	buht	撥
put, place	jài, fong	擠，放

put an advertise-ment in the paper	maaih goubaahk	賣告白
put aside	sàumàaih	收埋
put down	fongdài, jàidài	放低，擠低
put down in record	geiluhk, géiluhk	紀錄
put on (a hat, watch etc.)	daai	戴
put on (clothes)	jeuk	着
put out (fire or light)	sīk	熄
pyramid	gàmjihtaap	金字塔

Q

quack	wòhngluhk yīsāng	黃綠醫生
quail	ngāmchēun	鵪鶉
qualification	jìgaak	資格
qualified	gaujìgaak	夠資格
quality	jātdéi	質地
quantity	souleuhng	數量
quarrel	ngaaigāau	嗌咬
queen	wòhnghauh	皇后
quench thirsty	jíhot, gáaihot	止渴，解渴
question, problem	mahntàih	問題
queue, line up	pàaihdéui	排隊
quiet	jihng	靜
quietly, softly	jihngjíng (déi)	靜靜地
quite long (time)	géi noih	幾耐
quite, fairly	géi	幾
quiz, test	chāakyihm	測驗

R

rabbit		
race dragon-boats	tou (jái)	兔（仔）
radicals of	pàh lùhngsyùhn	扒龍船
	bousáu	部首
Chinese characters		
radio	sāuyàmgēi	收音機
radio station	dihntòih	電台
railroad	titlouh	鐵路
railroad station	fóchèjaahm	火車站
rain (n)	yúh	雨
rain (v)	lohkyúh	落雨
rainbow	chóihùhng	彩虹
raincoat	yúhlāu	雨褸
raise, elevate	tàihgòu	提高
raise, keep	yéuhng	養
raise one's hand	géuisáu	舉手
ransom	suhkgām	贖金
rash	chán	疹
rat, mouse	lóuhsyú	老鼠
rather, prefer	chìhngyún, nìhngyún	情願，寧願
rattan	tàhng	藤
rattan basket	tàhngláam	藤籃
reach, attain	daahtdou	達到
read (books)	táisyù	睇書
read aloud	duhk	讀
reader	duhkjé	讀者
ready	yuhbeihhóu	預備好
real, really	jànge	眞嘅
realize, achieve	sahtyihn	實現
reason	léihyàuh	理由
reason, cause	yùhnyān, yùhngu	緣因，緣故
reasonable	hahpléih	合理
receipt	sāugeui, sāutiuh	收據，收條
receive, get	jipdóu, sàudóu	接到，收到
receive baptism	sauhsái, líhngsái	受洗，領洗
receive education	sauh gaauyuhk	受教育

English	Romanization	Chinese
receiver	tèngtúng	聽筒
recently, lately	gahnlòih	近來
reception at a hotel	jipdoihchyu	接待處
reception room	wuihhaaksāt	會客室
receptionist	jipdoihyùhn	接待員
recognize	yihngdākchēut, yihngdāk	認得出，認得
recognize, admit	sìhngyihng	承認
recommend	tèuijin	推薦
record player	cheunggēi	唱機
record, make tape	luhkyām	錄音
recover (from sickness)	hóufàan	好番
recreation	yùhlohk	娛樂
recruit	jingping	徵聘
recuperate	yàuyéuhng	休養
red (colour)	hùhngsīk, hùhng	紅色，紅
reduce	gáam	減
refined, gentlemanlike	simàhn	斯文
reflection in water	dóuyíng	倒影
reform, reformation	góigaak	改革
refrigerator	syutgwaih	雪柜
refugee	naahnmàhn	難民
refuse	kéuihjyuht	拒絕
regarding..., as to...	jiyù	至於
register, registry	dānggei	登記
registered letter	gwahouhseun	掛號信
regret	hauhfui	後悔
regulation, rule	kwàigéui, kwàilaih, kwàijāk	規矩，規例，規則

relation, relationship	gwàanhaih	關係
relative	chānchìk	親戚
relax	fongsùng	放鬆
reliable, dependable	kaaudākjyuh	靠得住
relief, relieve	gaujai	救濟
relieve, stop (as pain, etc.)	jí	止
religion	jùnggaau, gaau	宗教，教
religious beilef	seunyéuhng	信仰
reluctant	míhnkéuhng	勉强
rely upon	jíyi	指意
remember	geidāk	記得
remind	tàihséng	提醒
remittance	wuihfún	滙款
remodel	góijòng	改裝
render service to...	waih . . . fuhkmouh	爲……服務
rent (n)	ngūkjòu, jòugàm	屋租，租金
rent (v)	jòu	租
rent paid in advance	seuhngkèihjòu	上期租
repair, fix	jíng	整
repay, requite	boudaap	報答
reply (by letter)	wùihseun	回信
report, make a report	bougou	報告
reporter, correspondent	geijé	記者
represent, representative	doihbíu	代表
reprove, rebuke	jaakfaht	責罰
reputation	mìhngyuh	名譽
request	chíngkàuh	請求
request, beg	kàuh	求
research	yìhngau	研究

resemble, look like	hóuchíh	好似
reserve, book	dehng	訂
reserve, keep	bóulàuh	保留
resident	gēuimàhn	居民
residential area	jyuhjaahkkēui	住宅區
respect	jyūnjuhng, jyunging	尊重，尊敬
respond, answer	ying	應
responsibility	jaakyahm	責任
responsible, in charge	fuhjaak	負責
rest, relax	táu, yāusīk	唞，休息
restaurant	jáugā, jáulàuh	酒家，酒樓
restaurant (Western food)	chāansāt	餐室
result, as a result	gitgwó	結果
results, achievement	sìhngjìk	成績
retail	lìhngsauh	零售
retire	teuiyāu	退休
return ticket	lòihwùihfèi	來回飛
return, pay back	wàahn	還
reveal (a secret)	sitlauh	洩漏
revenge	bousàuh	報仇
reviewer	pìhngleuhnyùhn	評論員
revolution	gaakmihng	革命
rhythm	jitjau	節奏
rib	lahkgwāt	肋骨
rice (cooked)	faahn	飯
rice (uncooked)	máih	米
rice ladle	faahnhok	飯殼
rice noodle	fán	粉
rice-field	tìhn	田
rich, wealthy	yáuhchín	有錢
rickshaw	chèjái, yàhnlihkchè	車仔，人力車
ride a bicycle	yáaidāanchè, cháaidāanchè	踹單車，踩單車
ride, to go by	chóh	坐

ridiculous	fòngmauh	荒謬
right (direction)	yauh	右
right, correct	ngāam	啱
ring	gaaijí	戒指
riot	bouhduhng	暴動
risk (n)	fùnghím	風險
risk (v)	mouhhím	冒險
river	hòh	河
road	louh	路
roast	sìu	燒
roast pork	sìuyuhk	燒肉
rock & roll music	yìuhgwánngohk	搖滾樂
rocking-chair	ngònlohkyí, yìuhyí	安樂椅，搖椅
roller-skates	syutkehk, làuhbīnghàaih	雪屐，溜冰鞋
romanization	lòhmáhpingyām	羅馬拼音
Rome	Lòhmáh	羅馬
roof	ngūkdéng, tìnpáang	屋頂，天棚
room	fóng	房
room or ward in a hospital	behngfóng	病房
roommate	tùhngfóng	同房
root (of plant)	gān	根
rope	síng	繩
rose	mùihgwai	玫瑰
rouge	yīnjì	胭脂
rough, coarse	chòu	粗
round, spherical	yùhn	圓
row, line	hòhng	行
row a boat	pàhtéhng	扒艇
ruby	hùhng bóusehk	紅寶石
rude	chòulóuh	粗魯
ruler (measure)	gaanchék	間尺
ruling queen	néuihwòhng	女皇
run, go fast	jáu	走
run a newspaper	baahnbougún	辦報館
run into trouble	johngbáan	撞板

94

| rust (n) | sau | 銹 |
| rust (v) | sāangsau | 生銹 |

S

sacrifice	hēisāng	犧牲
sad and lonely	chàilèuhng	淒涼
safe, safety	ngōnchyùhn	安全
safety-pin	kaujām	扣針
sail boat	fàahnsyùhn	帆船
salad	sāléut	沙律
salary	sānséui	薪水
salmon	sāammàhnyú	三文魚
salt	yìhm	鹽
salty	hàahm	鹹
same, alike	yātyeuhng	一樣
San Francisco	Gauhgāmsāan,	舊金山，
	Sàamfàahnsíh	三藩市
sand	sā	沙
sandals	lèuhnghàaih	涼鞋
sandwich	sàammàhnjih	三文治
sanitary	hahpwaihsāng	合衛生
Santa Claus	Singdaan-lóuhyàhn	聖誕老人
sapphire	làahm bóusehk	藍寶石
sardine	sādīnyú	沙甸魚
satisfy, satisfied	múhnyi	滿意
Saturday	láihbaailuhk	禮拜六
save, not spend	hāan	慳
save, rescue	gau	救
savings	jīkchūk	積蓄
saw (n)	geui	鋸
say, talk, speak, tell	góng	講
scald	luhkchàn	淥親
scales	bóng	磅

English	Romanization	Chinese
scallion	chūng	葱
scalp	tàuhpèih	頭皮
scandal	cháumàhn	醜聞
scar	nā, bàhàhn	挪，疤痕
scare	haak	嚇
scare to death	haakséi	嚇死
scared	gēng	驚
scarf	génggān	頸巾
scenery	fùnggíng	風景
schedule, time table	sìhgaanbíu	時間表
scholar	hohkjé	學者
scholarship	jéunghohkgām	獎學金
school	hohkhaauh	學校
school bus	haauhchè	校車
school of engineering	gùnghohkyún, gùngfò	工學院，工科
school of law	faathohkyún, faatfò	法學院，法科
school of liberal arts	màhnhohkyún, màhnfò	文學院，文科
school of natural science	léihhohkyún, léihfò	理學院，理科
school physician	haauhyī	校醫
school uniform	haauhfuhk	校服
schoolmate, classmate	tùhnghohk	同學
science	fōhohk	科學
scissors	gaaujín	較剪
scold	naauh	鬧
scope, sphere	faahnwàih	範圍
scratch (from a competition)	teuichēut	退出
scratch to relieve itching	ngàauhàhn	搯痕
scream, yell	ngaai	嗌
screw	lòhsī (dēng)	螺絲釘
screwdriver	lòhsīpāi	螺絲批

sea	hói	海
sea gull	hóingāu	海鷗
sea shell	hínhok	蜆殼
sea water	hàahmséui, hóiséui	鹹水，海水
sea-horse	hóimáh	海馬
sea-sick	wàhnlohng	暈浪
seafood (dried)	hóiméi	海味
seafood (fresh)	hóisīn	海鮮
seal, chop	tòuhjēung	圖章
sealed letter	màaihháuseun	埋口信
search	wán, cháau	揾，抄
seashore	hóibīn	海邊
season	gwaijit	季節
seat	wái	位
secluded, quiet	yàujihng	幽靜
second	daihyih	第二
second class	yihdáng	二等
second handed	yihsáu	二手
secret, secretly	beimaht	祕密
secretary	beisyù	祕書
see a movie	táihei	睇戲
see someone off	sunghàhng	送行
see, perceive	táigin	睇見
seed	júngjí	種子
seesaw	yìuhyìuhbáan	搖搖板
select	gáan	揀
self support	jihlahp	自立
self, alone	jihgéi, jihgēi	自己
self-contradictory	jih-sēung-màauh-téuhn	自相予盾
selfish	jih sī	自私
sell	maaih	賣
semester	hohkkèih	學期
send, dispatch	paai	派
send, post	gei	寄
send a telegram	dá dihnbou	打電報
senses	jigok	知覺

English	Romanization	Chinese
separate	fànhòi	分開
separate, part	fànsáu	分手
September	Gáuyuht	九月
serious, important	gányiu	緊要
serious, grave	yìhmjuhng	嚴重
seriously	yihngjàn	認眞
servant, worker	gùngyàhn	工人
serve	fuhkmouh	服務
serve, wait on	fuhksih	服侍
service charge	siujeung, (fuhkmouh- fai)	小賬 （服務費）
set, inlay with	sèung	鑲
set up, establish	ginlahp	建立
seven	chāt	七
Seven up	Chāthéi	七喜
sew button on	dēngnáu	釘鈕
sew by machine	chè	車
sew with needle and thread	lyùhn	聯
sewing machine	yīchè	衣車
sex	singbiht	性別
shade (v)	jējyuh	遮住
shadow	ying	影
shake hands	ngāaksáu, āaksáu	握手
shall, will, may	wúih	會
shallow, light	chín	淺
shampoo (n)	sáitàuhséui	洗頭水
shampoo (v)	sáitàuh	洗頭
Shanghai	Seuhnghói	上海
shape, form	yìhngjohng	形狀
share (n)	fahn	份
share (v)	fàn	分
share a table (in a restaurant)	daaptói	搭枱
shareholder	gúdùng	股東

shark	sāyùh	鯊魚
sharp	leih	利
sharpener (for pencil)	yùhnbātpáau	鉛筆刨
Shatin	Sātìhn	沙田
shave	tai	剃
shave beard	taisōu	剃鬚
she, her	kéuih	佢
sheep	yèuhng	羊
sheet (for a bed)	chòhngdāan	床單
ship, boat	syùhn	船
shirt	sēutsāam	恤衫
shiver	dá láahngjan	打冷震
shoe lace	hàaihdáai	鞋帶
shoe polish	hàaihyáu	鞋油
shoes	hàaih	鞋
shop	poutáu	舖頭
short (in length)	dyún	短
short (not tall)	ngái	矮
shoulder	boktàuh	膊頭
shout at	hot	喝
show, performance	bíuyín	表演
shower, bathe	chùnglèuhng	冲凉
shower-head	fāsá	花灑
shrewd	jēng	精
shrewd (with money)	wúih dásyunpùhn	會打算盤
shrimp	hā	蝦
shrink (of cloth)	sūkséui	縮水
shut	sāanmàaih	閂埋
shut up!	máihchòuh	咪嘈
shy	pacháu	怕醜
sickness, be sick	behng	病
side	bīn, bihn	邊
sidewalk, pavement	hàahngyàhnlouh	行人路
sigh	taanhei	嘆氣

sign, signature	chìmméng	簽名
signboard	jīupàaih	招牌
significance	yiyih	意義
silent	jihng	靜
silk	sī	絲
silver color	ngàhnsīk	銀色
silverware	dōuchā, ngàhnhei	刀叉，銀器
simple	gáandāan	簡單
simplified character	gáanbātjih, gaantáijih	簡筆字，簡體字
since, because	geiyìhn	既然
since childhood	jihsai	自細
sing	cheung	唱
sing (a song)	cheunggō	唱歌
singer	gōsáu, gōsīng	歌手，歌星
single room	dāanyàhnfóng	單人房
sisters	jímuih	姊妹
sit, drop in	chóh	坐
sit down	chóhdài	坐低
sit up	chóh héisàn	坐起身
six	luhk	六
size	chekmáh	尺碼
skating-rink	làuhbīngchèuhng	溜冰場
skeleton	fūlòuhgwāt	骷髏骨
skill, trade	sáungaih	手藝
skin	pèih	皮
skirt	kwàhn, bunjihtkwàhn	裙，半截裙
sky, heaven	tìn	天
sleep, go to bed	fangaau, fan	瞓覺，瞓
sleeping pill	ōnmìhnyeuhk	安眠藥
sleepy	ngáahnfan	眼瞓
sleeve	jauh	袖
slide (n)	waahndāngpin	幻燈片
slightly	sáauwàih	稍爲
slipper	tōháai	拖鞋
slippery, smooth	waaht	滑
sloping, slanting	che	斜

sloppy	séuipèih	水皮
slow	maahn	慢
slowly, gradually	maahnmáan	慢慢
small, little	sai	細
small amount, little bit	sēsíu	些少
small boat	téhng	艇
small size	saimáh	細碼
smallpox	tìnfà	天花
smart	lēk	叻
smell (n)	meih gok	味覺
smell (v)	màhn	聞
smile	siu	笑
smog	yīnmouh	烟霧
smoke (n)	yīn	煙
smoke (v)	sihkyīn	食煙
smoothly, successfully	seuhnleih	順利
smuggle, smuggling	jáusī	走私
snack	síusihk, háulahpsāp	小食，口立濕
snail	wòngàuh	蝸牛
snake	sèh	蛇
sneak away	sùngyàhn	鬆人
sneeze	dá hātchī	打乞嗤
snore (n)	beihhòhnsēng	鼻鼾聲
snore (v)	chébeihhòhn	扯鼻鼾
snow (n)	syut	雪
snow (v)	lohksyut	落雪
so called	sówaih	所謂
so forth, etc.	dángdáng	等等
so so, not bad	syunhaih gám lā	算係咁啦
so, such	gam	咁
soap	fàangáan	番梘
soccer	jūkkàuh	足球
social engagement	yingchàuh	應酬
social security	séhwúih bóujeung	社會保障

social worker	séhgùng, séhwúihgùngjokjé	社工，社會工作者
society, community	séhwúi	社會
sociologist	séhwúihhohkgā	社會學家
sociology	séhwúihhohk	社會學
soda	heiséui	汽水
sofa	sōfá	梳化
soft	yúhn	軟
soft-hearted	sàmchèuhng yúhn	心腸軟
soldier	gwànyàhn	軍人
solicitor, lawyer	leuhtsī	律師
solicitor's office	leuhtsīlàuh	律師樓
solo	duhk cheung	獨唱
solve, settle	gáaikyut	解決
some, somewhat	yáuhdī	有啲
sometimes	yáuhsìh	有時
son	jái	仔
song	gō	歌
soon, immediately	jauhlàih	就嚟
sooner or later, eventually	chìhjóu	遲早
soprano	néuih gōuyām	女高音
sorrowful, melancholy	chàicháam	凄慘
sorry	deuimjyuh	對唔住
sound, voice	sìngyàm	聲音
soup (thick)	gāng	羹
soup (thin)	tòng	湯
soup ladle	tònghok	湯殼
soupspoon	tònggàng	湯羹
sour	syùn	酸
south	nàahm	南
South America	Nàahmméihjàu	南美洲
southeast	dùngnàahm	東南

Southeastern Asia	Nàahmyéung, Dùngnàahmnga	南洋，東南亞
southwest	sàinàahm	西南
souvenir	géinihmbán	紀念品
soy sauce	sihyàuh, chāuyáu	豉油，抽油
space-ship	taaihùngsyùhn	太空船
space-shuttle	taaihùngchyūnsōgēi	太空穿梭機
Spain	Sāibāanngàh	西班牙
spatula	wohkcháan	鑊鏟
speak	góng	講
special, unusual	dahkbiht	特別
specialized, exclusively	jyūnmún, jyūnmùhn	專門
specially, particularly	jyūndāng, dahkdāng	專登，特登
speculative	tàuhgèi	投機
speed boat	faaitéhng	快艇
speedily, in a hurry	gónjyuh	趕住
speeding	hòifaaichè, chìuchùk	開快車，超速
spend (money)	sái	洗
spider	jījyū	蜘蛛
spinal cord	jekséuih	脊髓
spirit, cheerful	jìngsàhn	精神
spit	tou tàahm	吐痰
spoken language or dialect	wa	話
sponge-cake	daahngōu	蛋糕
spoon	chìhgāng	匙羹
sport shoes	bōhàaih, wahnduhnghàaih	波鞋，運動鞋
spring	chēuntin	春天
spring (water source)	panchyùhn, chyùhn	噴泉，泉
spring-board	tiubáan	跳板
spring-water	chyùhnséui	泉水
square	fōng, seifōng	方，四方

square (an open area)	gwóngchèuhng	廣場
square kilometer	fōnggùngléih	方公里
squirrel	chùhngsyú	松鼠
St. Valentine's Day	chìhngyàhnjit	情人節
stab, pierce	gāt	刮
stadium	wahnduhngchèuhng	運動場
staff member	jīkyùhn	職員
stainless steel	bātsaugong	不銹鋼
stairs	làuhtāi	樓梯
stall	dongháu	檔口
stamp	yàuhpiu, sihdāam	郵票，士担
stand	kéih	企
stand in a long line	pàaihchèuhnglùhng	排長龍
stand in line	pàaihdéui	排隊
stand up	kéihhéisàn	企起身
standard, level	séuijéun	水準
standard, model	bīujéun	標準
star	sīng, sīngkàuh	星，星球
stare at	mohngjyuh	望住
start, begin	héisáu, hòichí	起首，開始
start a journey	hèichìhng	起程
start away (ship, train, etc.)	hòisàn	開身
state (of the United States)	jāu	州
state of mind	sàmléih	心理
statement on income tax	seuidāan	稅單
status, rank	deihwaih	地位
stay	jyuh, dauhlàuh	住，逗留
stay in hospital	làuhyī	留醫
stay overnight	gwoyeh	過夜
steak	ngàuhpá	牛扒
steal	tàu	偷

steam (n)	jìnghei	蒸氣
steam (v)	jìng	蒸
steel	gong	鋼
steel bar	gonggān	鋼筋
steering wheel	táaih	軚
step by step	yātbouhyātbouh	一步一步
sterilize	siuduhk	消毒
Sterling pound	Yìngbóng, Yìngbohng	英鎊
stewed	mān	炆
still	yìhngyìhn	仍然
stir fry, saute	cháau	炒
stock market	gúsíh	股市
stocking, sock	maht	襪
stomach	waih	胃
stomach upset	fáanwaih	反胃
stomachache	tóuhtung, waihtung	肚痛，胃痛
stone, rock	sehk, sehktàuh	石，石頭
stoop down and squat	màudài, màu	跍低，跍
stop, halt	tìhngjí, tìhng	停止，停
stop, station	jaahm	站
stop (someone to do something)	jójí	阻止
stop or relieve pain	jítung	止痛
store, shop	poutáu	舖頭
store room	chyúhmahtsāt, sihdōfóng	儲物室，士多房
storm	daaihfùngyúh	大風雨
story	gújái	古仔
stove, furnace	fólòuh	火爐
stove (electric)	dihnlòuh	電爐
stove (gas)	mùihheilòuh	煤氣爐
stove (L.P. gas)	sehkyàuhheilòuh	石油氣爐
straight ahead	yātjihk	一直
straight forward, open-hearted	sóngjihk	爽直

strainer (for drying)	sāaugēi	筲箕
strainer (for frying)	jaaulēi	炸籬
strainer (tea)	chàhgaak	茶隔
strange, puzzling	chēutkèih	出奇
strange, special	dahkbiht, dākyi	特別，得意
stranger	sāangbóuyàhn	生步人
street	gāai	街
stretch out, stick out	sàn	伸
strict	yìhm	嚴
strike	bahgùng	罷工
strokes of characters	bātwaahk	筆劃
stroll	saanbouh	散步
structure	kaujouh	構造
stubborn	wàahngu	頑固
student	hohksāang	學生
student studying abroad	làuhhohksāang	留學生
study (books)	duhksyù	讀書
study abroad	làuhhohk	留學
study room	syùfóng	書房
stuffy	ngaiguhk	翳焗
stupid	chéun, bahn	蠢，笨
style, pattern	fún, fúnsīk	款，款式
stylish	sìhhìng, sìhfún	時興，時款
subject, field	fōmuhk	科目
subscribe	dehng, dihng	訂，定
subtract, reduce	gáam	減
success, successful	sìhnggùng	成功
successively	lìhnhei, yātlìhn	連氣，一連
such as...and the like	hóuchih ... jiléui	好似……之類
suddenly	fātyìhn, fātyìhngāan	忽然，忽然間

suffer	sauhfú	受苦
suffer injury, be wounded	sauhsēung	受傷
suffer lose, be cheated	sihtdái	蝕底
sufficient	chùngjūk	充足
sugar	tòhng	糖
sugar cane	je	蔗
suggest, propose	tàihyíh	提議
suitable, fit	hahpsīk, sīkhahp	合適，適合
suitcase	pèihgīp	皮喼
suite	toufóng	套房
summer	hahtìn, yihttìn	夏天，熱天
summer vacation	syúga	暑假
summit	sāandéng	山頂
sun (n)	yahttáu, taaiyèuhng	日頭，太陽
sun (v)	saai	曬
sun glasses	taaiyèuhng ngáahn-géng	太陽眼鏡
sun-bathing	saai taaiyèuhng	曬太陽
Sunday	láihbaaihyaht, láihbaai	禮拜日，禮拜
Sunday school	Jyúyahthohk	主日學
sunflower	heungyahtkwàih	向日葵
sunshine	yahttáu	日頭
superficially	biumihnseuhng	表面上
superfluous	dòyùh	多餘
supermarket	chiukāpsihchèuhng	超級市場
supervise, supervisor	gāamdūk	監督
support	jichìh	支持
support (with hand or hands)	fùh	扶
suppose, think	yíhwàih	以為
sure	yātdihng	一定
surely will, definitely	yātyù	一於

surgical operation	sáuseuht	手術
surgical department	ngoihfō	外科
surname	sing	姓
surprise	gingkèih	驚奇
surround	wàihjyuh	圍住
suspect, presume	siyìh	思疑
suspend	tìhngdeuhn	停頓
suspicious	hóyìh	可疑
swallow (n)	yin(jí)	燕（子）
swallow (v)	tàn	吞
swear (an oath)	saihyuhn	誓願
sweat, perspire	chēut hohn	出汗
sweater	lāangsāam	冷衫
sweep	sou	掃
sweep floor	soudeih	掃地
sweet	tìhm	甜
sweet potato, yam	fàansyú	番薯
swell, swelling	júng	腫
swift	faaijit	快捷
swim	yàuhséui	游水
swimmers' raft	fàuhtòih	浮台
swimming cap	wìhngmóu	泳帽
swimming pool	wìhngchìh	泳池
swimming suit	(yàuh)wìhngyī	（游）泳衣
swing (for kids)	chāuchin	鞦韆
switch (electrical)	dihnjai	電掣
switch off	sik, sāan	熄，閂
switch on	hòi	開
sympathize	tùhngchìhng	同情
sympathy	tùhngchìhngsàm	同情心
symphony	gāau héung ngohk	交響樂
system	jaidouh	制度

T

T-shirt	Tīsēut	T恤
table, desk	tói	枱
table cloth	tóibou	枱布
tail	méih	尾
tailor	chòihfúng	裁縫
Taiwan	Tòihwāan	台灣
take, bring	daai	帶
take, carry (by hand)	nīk, nīng	搦，拎
take...for example	hóuchíh ... gám	好似……咁
take a chance	bok	搏
take a rest	táuháh	唞吓
take a shower or bath	chùnglèuhng	沖涼
take a walk	saanbouh	散步
take afternoon nap	fanngaangaau	瞓晏覺
take care, bring up, (baby, kid)	chau	湊
take care of, manage	dáléih	打理
take good care	bóujuhng	保重
take in, receive	sàu	收
take it easy	m̀sái gam gánjèung	唔駛咁緊張
take lead, lead	líhngdouh	領導
take off	chèuih	除
take off (as an airplane)	héifèi	起飛
take one's time	maahnmáan	慢慢
take order (in business)	jipsāangyi	接生意
take photograph	yíngséung	影相
take temperature	taamyiht	探熱

take turns	lèuhnláu	輪流
take X-ray	jiu X-gwòng	照X光
talcum powder	sóngsànfán	爽身粉
talent	tìnchòih	天才
talented persons	yàhnchòih	人才
talk back, answer back	bok	駁
talkative (negative meaning)	dòjéui	多嘴
talkative (positive meaning)	gihntàahm	健談
tall, high	gòu	高
tangerine	gāt	桔
Taoist, Taoism	Douhgaau	道教
tap, faucet	séuihàuh	水喉
tape	luhkyāmdáai	錄音帶
tape recorder	luhkyāmgēi	錄音機
taste (v)	simeihdouh	試味道
tasty, delicious	hóumeih(douh)	好味（道）
taxi	dīksí	的士
taxing, fatiguing	sànfú	辛苦
tea	chàh	茶
tea kettle	chàhbōu	茶煲
tea leaf	chàhyihp	茶葉
tea party	chàhwúi	茶會
tea-table, coffee table	chàhgēi	茶几
teach	gaau	教
teach (at school)	gaausyù	教書
teacher	lóuhsī, gaauyùhn	老師，教員
teakwood	yáumuhk	柚木
teapot	chàhwú	茶壺
tear (n)	ngáahnleuih	眼淚
tear (v)	sìlaahn	撕爛
tear down	chaak	拆

tear, rip, open	chaak	拆
teaspoon	chàhgāng	茶羹
technology	geihseuht	技術
tedious	mòuhlìuh	無聊
telegram	dihnbou	電報
telegraph office	dihnbougúk	電報局
telephone	dihnwá	電話
telephone booth	dihnwá tíng	電話亭
telephone directory	dihnwábóu	電話簿
telephone extension	fāngēi	分機
telephone operator	jipsinsāng	接線生
telephone outside line	gāaisin	街線
telescope	mohngyúhngeng	望遠鏡
television	dihnsihgēi	電視機
tell	góng	講
tell, order	giu	叫
tell a lie	góngdaaihwah	講大話
temper, disposition	singchìhng, pèihhei	性情，脾氣
temperature	wāndouh	溫度
fahrenheit	wahsih	華氏
centigrade	sipsih	攝氏
temple	jí, míu	寺，廟
temporarily	jaahmsih	暫時
ten	sahp	十
ten percent	yātsìhng	一成
ten thousand	maahn	萬
tenant	jyuhhaak, jòuhaak	住客，租客
tennis	móhngkàuh	網球
tenor	nàahm gòuyàm	男高音
terminus	júngjaahm	總站
terrifying, frightening	dākyàhngèng	得人驚

test, quiz	chāakyihm	測驗
text book	gaaufōsyù	教科書
textile factory	jīkjouhchóng	織造廠
Thailand	Taaigwok	泰國
thank you	dòjeh	多謝
Thanksgiving day	Gámyànjit	感恩節
that	gógo	嗰個
The Americas (North and South)	Méihjàu	美洲
the East	Dùngfòng	東方
the first time	chòchi	初次
the Gospel	fūkyam	福音
The Great Wall	(Maahn-léih)-chèuhng -sìhng	（萬里）長城
the other, the rest	kèihtàge, kèihyùhge	其他嘅，其餘嘅
the same day	jīkyaht	即日
the Savior	Gausaijyú	救世主
the West	sāifòng	西方
the whole world	chyùhnsaigaai	全世界
The yellow pages (classified index in the telephone directory	wòhngyihp	黃頁
theatre	heiyún	戲院
then, in such a way	gámyéung	咁樣
then, thereupon	yùsih	於是
there	gósyu, gódouh	嗰處，嗰度
therefore	sóyíh, yànchí	所以，因此
thermometer (measuring temperature)	hòhnsyúbíu	寒暑表
thermometer (taking temperature)	taamyihtjām	探熱針

thermos bottle	nyúhnséuiwú	暖水壺
these	nīdī	呢啲
thesis, essay	leuhnmàhn, leuhnmán	論文
they, them	kéuihdeih	佢哋
thick	háuh	厚
thick (of high density)	giht	杰
thief, bandit	chaahk, cháak	賊
thigh	daaihbéi	大髀
thin (not fat)	sau	瘦
thin (not thick)	bohk	薄
thin (of low density)	hèi	稀
thing	yéh	嘢
think	nám/lám	惗
think of, think about	séung	想
thirst, thirsty	háuhot, génghot	口渴，頸渴
thirty	sàamsahp	三十
this (here)	nī	呢
this morning	gàmjìujóu, gàmjìu	今朝早，今朝
this year	gàmnin, gàmnihn	今年
thorough, careful	jàudou	周到
those	gódī	嗰啲
those days	gópáai	嗰排
thought, thinking, ideology	siséung	思想
thoughtful, considerate	yáuhsàm, saisàm	有心，細心
thousand	chìn	千
thrash board	fàuhbáan	浮板
thread, wire, cord, string	sin	線
three	sàam	三
throat	hàuhlùhng	喉嚨
throw light on	jiu	照
throw, discard	dám	扰

113

thumb	sáujígùng, móuhjí	手指公，姆指
thumb through (a book)	kín	掀
thundering and lightening	hàahnglèuih sín dihn	行雷閃電
Thursday	láihbaaisei	禮拜四
ticket	piu, fèi	票，飛
tickle	jīt	噉
tidy up (things)	jāpsahp	執拾
tidy up a bedroom	jāpfóng	執房
tie up (things)	bóngjyuh, jaatjyuh	綁住，紮住
tiger	lóuh fú	老虎
tight	gán	緊
tiles	gāaijyūn	階磚
time (duration)	sihgaan	時間
time (occasion)	chi	次
timid	m̀gaudáam, saidáam	唔夠膽，細膽
tin (metal)	sek	錫
tip, gratuity	tīpsí	貼士
tired	guih	癐
tired, bored	yim	厭
tissue	jígàn	紙巾
to be	haih	係
toast	hongmihnbāau, dōsí	炕麵包，多士
toaster	dōsilòuh	多士爐
tobacco	yīnchóu	煙草
today	gàmyaht	今日
toe	geukjí	腳指
together	yātchái, yātchàih	一齊
together with	tùhng, tùhngmàaih	同，同埋
toilet	sáisáugāan, chisó	洗手間，廁所
toilet cleaner (liquid)	gitchiyihk	潔廁液
toilet cleaner (powder)	gitchifán	潔廁粉
toilet tissue	chijí	廁紙
tolerate	(yùhng) yán	（容）忍

tomato	fàanké	番茄
tomato juice	fàankéjāp	番茄汁
tomorrow	tìngyaht	聽日
tomorrow morning	tìngjiujóu, tìngjiu	聽朝早，聽朝
tomorrow night	tìngmáahn	聽晚
tones	sìngdiuh	聲調
tongue	leih	脷
tonight	gàmmaahn	今晚
tonsillitis	bíntòuhsin faatyìhm	扁桃腺發炎
tonsils	hàuhwát, bíntòuhsin	喉核，扁桃腺
too, also	dōu, yihkdōu	都，亦都
too, excessively	taai	太
too bad! what a mess!	baih la!	弊嘞！
too much trouble	faisih	費事
tooth	ngàh	牙
tooth paste	ngàhgòu	牙膏
tooth picks	ngàhchìm	牙簽
toothache	ngàhtung	牙痛
toothbrush	ngàhcháat	牙刷
toothpick-holder	ngàhchìmtúng	牙簽桶
top	déng	頂
top, above, on	seuhngbihn	上便
total, altogether	yātguhng	一共
totally	júngguhng	總共
touch (v)	mó, mō	摸
tour (v)	yàuhláahm, yàuh	遊覽，遊
tour around the world	wàahnyàuh saigaai	環遊世界
tour group	léuihhàhngtyùhn	旅行團
tourism	léuihyàuh sihyihp	旅遊事業
tourist	yàuhhaak	旅客
tourist coach	léuihyàuh bāsí	旅遊巴士
tow	tō	拖
toward (the direction of), face	heung	向

115

towel	sáugán	手巾
traction engine	tōchè	拖車
tractor	tōlāaigēi	拖拉機
tradition, traditional	chyùhntúng	傳統
traffic	gāautùng	交通
traffic jam	sākchè	塞車
traffic sign	gāautùng bīuji	交通標誌
tragic, pitiable	cháam	慘
train	fóchè	火車
train, training	fanlihn	訓練
tram-car	dihnchè	電車
transform into	binsèhng, binsìhng	變成
transformation	binfa	變化
translate	yihk, fàanyihk	譯，翻譯
translate into (other language)	yihksìhng	譯成
translation	fàanyihk	翻譯
transport	wahn	運
transportation system	gāautùng	交通
travel, trip	léuihhàhng	旅行
travel agency	léuihhàhngséh	旅行社
traveller's check	léuihhàhng jìpiu	旅行支票
travelling expenses	léuihfai, séuigeuk	旅費，水脚
tray	tokpún	托盤
treat (act toward)	deui	對
tree	syuh	樹
tree leaf	syuhyihp	樹葉
tribe, race	júngjuhk	種族
tribulation	fúnaahn	苦難
tricycle	sàamlèuhnchè	三輪車
trouble	màhfàahn	麻煩
trousers	fu	褲
truck	fochè	貨車
true, real	jàn	眞

116

true, reliable	koksaht	確實
trumpet	labā	喇叭
trust	seunyahm	信任
trustworthy	seundākgwo	信得過
try, taste	si	試
tuberculosis	fai behng	肺病
Tuesday	láihbaaiyih	禮拜二
tuition	hohkfai	學費
tumor	láu	瘤
tunnel	seuihdouh	隧道
tunnel bus	seuihdouh bāsí	隧道巴士
tunnel fee	seuihdouhfai	隧道費
turkey	fógāi	火鷄
turn on	hòi	開
turn one's head	nihngjyuntàuh	擰轉頭
turn, make a turn	jyun	轉
turnoff	sĭk, sàan	熄，閂
turtle neck	jēunléhng	樽領
TV movie	dihnsihkehk	電視劇
TV set	dihnsihgēi	電視機
TV station	dihnsihtòih	電視台
twenty	yihsahp	二十
twin	mā	孖
twin boys	mājái	孖仔
twin girls	mānéui	孖女
twist	náu	扭
two	yih	二
type (v)	dájih	打字
typewriter	dájihgēi	打字機
typhoon	dáfùng	打風
typhoon shelter	beihfùngtòhng	避風塘
typhoon signal	fùngkàuh	風球
typist	dájihyùhn	打字員

U

U.S. dollar	Méihgàm	美金
U.S.S.R., Soviet Russia	Sōulyùhn, Sōungòh	蘇聯，蘇俄
ugly	cháuyéung	醜樣
ulcer	waihkwúiyèuhng	胃潰瘍
umbrella	jē	遮
unbutton	gáaináu	解鈕
unceasingly	bātdyuhn	不斷
unconsciously, unknowingly	bātjibātgok	不知不覺
under, underneath	hahbihn	下便
under...	hái ... hahbihn	喺……下便
under nourished	yìhngyéuhng bātlèuhng	營養不良
underpants	dáifu	底褲
undershirt	dáisāam	底衫
underskirt, slip	dáikwahn	底裙
understand	mìhngbaahk, líuhgáai	明白，了解
underwear	noihyīfu, dáisāamfu	內衣褲，底衫褲
undress, take off	chèuih	除
unforeseen loss	yingoih syúnsāt	意外損失
unified	tyùhngit	團結
uniform	jaifuhk	制服
uniformly (for all)	yātleuht	一律
unify	túngyāt	統一
unintentionally	m̀gokyi	唔覺意
unit	dāanwái	單位
United Nations	Lyùhnhahpgwok	聯合國
university, college	daaihhohk	大學
unless, only if	chèuihfēi	除非
unmanageable	gáaum̀dihm	搞唔惦
unreasonable	móuhdouhléih	冇道理
unsealed letter	hòiháuseun	開口信
untie	gáai	解

up to now, until now	yātheung, yātheung dōu	一向，一向都
upright, straight	jeng	正
upset, irritated	sàmfàahn	心煩
upstairs	làuhseuhng	樓上
urban district	sìhkēui	市區
urge, rush	chèui	催
urgent	gángāp	緊急
urine	liuh, siubihn	尿，小便
us	ngóhdeih	我哋
usage	yuhngtòuh	用途
use	yuhng	用
used up	yuhngsaai	用曬
useful, helpful	yáuhyuhng	有用
useless	móuhyuhng	冇用
usher, greet	jīufù	招呼
usually	tūngsèuhng	通常
utensil	yuhnggeuih	用具
utter, say (something)	chēutsēng	出聲

V

vacation	fongga	放假
vacation house, villa	bihtseuih	別墅
vaccum cleaner	kāpchàhngēi	吸塵機
valuable	jihkchín	值錢
value	gajihk	價值
various	goksīk gokyeuhng	各式各樣
vase	fājēun	花樽
vaseline	fàahnsihlàhm	凡士林
vault, safe	gaapmaahn	夾萬
vegetables	choi	菜
vein	jihngmahk	靜脈
venereal disease	singbehng	性病

very	hóu	好
very fond of	hóu jùngyi	好中意
vicinity, near-by	jógán, fuhgahn	左近，附近
victim	sauhhoihyàhn	受害人
Victoria Peak	Chékèihsāandéng	扯旗山頂
victory	singleih	勝利
video cassette	luhkyíngdáai	錄影帶
video cassette recorder	luhkyínggēi	錄影機
view, scenery	fùnggíng	風景
village	chyūn, hēungchyūn	村，鄉村
vinegar	chou, jitchou	醋，浙醋
violet	jilòhlàahn	紫羅蘭
violin	siutàihkàhm	小提琴
virtue, moral	douhdāk	道德
visa	chimjing	簽證
viscid, thick	giht	澔
vision	sih gok	視覺
visit (a person)	taam	探
visit (a place)	chàamgùn	參觀
visit a patient	taambehng	探病
visitor, guest	yàhnhaak	人客
visual acuity	ngáahnlihk	眼力
vocabulary	chìhwuih	詞滙
voice, sound	sēng	聲
volley ball	pàaihkàuh	排球
volunteer (v)	jihyuhn	自願
vomit	ngáu, áu	嘔

W

wage	yàhngùng	人工
waist	yīu	腰
wait, wait for	dáng	等
wait a moment	dángyātjahn	等一陣
wait on (upon)	fuhksih	服侍

waiter	fógei	伙記
waiting room	wuihhaaksāt	會客室
waiting room (in a doctor's office)	hauhchánsāt	候診室
waiting room (in an airport)	hauhgēisāt	候機室
wake (others) up	giuséng	叫醒
wake up	séng	醒
wake up from dream	faatséngmuhng	發醒夢
walk, work (of watches, cars, etc.)	hàahng	行
walk by	hàahnggwo	行過
wall	chèuhng	牆
wall, fence	wàihchèuhng	圍牆
wallet, purse	ngàhnbāau	銀包
want	yiu	要
wardrobe	yīgwaih	衣柜
warm	nyúhn	暖
warship	jinlaahm	戰艦
wash	sái	洗
wash basin	mihnpún	面盤
wash-room, toilet	chisó, sáisáugāan	厠所，洗手間
washing machine	sáiyīgèi	洗衣機
waste	sāai	嘥
waste-paper basket	jihjílō	字紙簍
watch (n)	bīu	錶
watch (v)	tái	睇
watch out	gujyuh	顧住
water (n)	séui	水
water (v)	làhm	淋
water bill	séuifai	水費
water tank	séuisēung	水箱
water-colour	séuichói	水彩

water-ski	waahtséui	滑水
waterfall	buhkbou	瀑布
watermelon	sāigwà	西瓜
waterproof	fòhngséuige	防水嘅
watery, thin	hèi	稀
wave (n)	lohng	浪
wax (v)	dálaahp	打蠟
way, method	fōngfaat, faatjí	方法，法子
way, route	louh	路
we, us	ngóhdeih	我哋
weak	yeuhk	弱
weakness	hèuiyeuhk, yúhnyeuhk	虛弱，軟弱
wear (glasses, hat etc.)	daai	戴
wear, dress	jeuk	着
wear a necktie	dátāai	打吠
wear a scarf	laahm génggàn	攬頸巾
wearing a long face	báanhéi go mihn	板起個面
weather	tìnhei	天氣
weave	jīk	織
wedding cake	láihbéng	禮餅
wedding ceremony	fànláih	婚禮
wedding gown	gitfàn láihfuhk	結婚禮服
Wednesday	láihbaaisāam	禮拜三
week	láihbaai, sìngkèih	禮拜，星期
week by week	juhkgo láihbaai	逐個禮拜
weep	haam	喊
weigh	bohng	磅
weigh (by Chinese scale)	ching	稱
welcome	fùnyìhng	歡迎
welfare	fūkleih	福利
well (n)	jéng	井
well informed	sìusìk lìhngtùng	消息靈通
well known	chēutméng	出名
well off, rich	yáuhchín	有錢

west	sāi	西
West Germany	Sāidāk	西德
Western calendar	sāilihk	西曆
western food	sāichāan	西餐
Western style	sāisīk	西式
Western suit	sāijōng	西裝
Westerner	sāiyàhn, gwáilóu	西人，鬼佬
wet	sāp	濕
whale	kìhngyùh	鯨魚
wharf	máhtàuh	碼頭
what	māt, mātyéh	乜，乜嘢
What a coincidence!	jànhaih ngāam la!	真係啱嘞！
what a waste!	sāaisaai la!	嘥晒嘞！
when (at the time that)	... gójahnsi	嗰陣時
when?, at what time?	géisí, géisìh	幾時
where?	bīnsyu, bīndouh	邊處，邊度
which?	bīn	邊
whisky	wāisihgéi	威士忌
whistle (n)	ngàhngāi, saaují	銀雞，哨子
whistle (v)	chèuiháusaau	吹口哨
white	baahksīk, baahk	白色，白
white wash	fùiséui	灰水
who's?	bīngo ge	邊個嘅
who?, whom?	bīngo	邊個
whole day	sèhngyaht	成日
wholeheartedly	jeuhn-sàm-jeuhn-lihk	盡心盡力
wholesale	pāifaat	批發
why?	dímgáai	點解
why should ...?	hòhbīt, sáimāt	何必，駛乜
wide, loose (dress)	fut	闊
widow	gwáfúh	寡婦
wife	taaitáai, lóuhpòh	太太，老婆
wig	gáfaat	假髮

123

wild animals, beast	yéhsau	野獸
will (personal)	wàihjūk	遺囑
will, shall	wúih	會
will be in trouble	m̀dākdihm	唔得掂
willing to	háng	肯
win	yèhng	贏
win a prize	dākjéung	得獎
wind, breeze	fùng	風
windbreaker	fùngyì, fùnglàu	風衣，風褸
windmill	fùngchè	風車
window	chēung, chēungmún	窗，窗門
window curtain	chēunglím	窗簾
windy	daaihfùng	大風
wine	jáu	酒
wine bottle	jáujēun	酒樽
winepot	jáuwùh	酒壺
wink, blink	jáam	眨
wink, in a wink	jáamngáahn	眨眼
winter	dūngtin, láahngtin	冬天，冷天
winter recess	hòhn'ga	寒假
wipe	maat	抹
wisdom	jiwai	智慧
wise	chùngmìhng	聰明
wish (well)	jūk	祝
wish or congratulate in advance	yuhjūk	預祝
wish to, would like to	séung	想
wish, desire	yuhnmohng	願望
with one's own hands	chànsáu	親手
with regard to	gwāanyù	關於
with respect to, in regard to	deui (yù)	對（於）

124

without authorization	sìjih	私自
witness	jingyàhn, muhkgìkjé	證人，目擊者
wok (Chinese cooking pan)	wohk	鑊
woman	néuihyán	女人
wood	muhk	木
woods	syuhlàhm	樹林
wool	yèuhngmòuh	羊毛
woolen material	yúng	絨
Worcestershire sauce	gìpjāp	喼汁
word, character (written word)	jih	字
work (v)	jouhsih	做事
work hard	nóulihk	努力
workshop	gùngchèuhng	工場
world	saigaai	世界
world war	saigaaidaaihjin	世界大戰
worm, insects	chùhng	蟲
worried	baingai	閉翳
worry about, worried	dāamsàm	擔心
worship	baai	拜
worthwhile	jihkdāk	值得
wound (n)	sēungháu	傷口
wrangle, strive	jāang	爭
wrap	bāau	包
wrist	sáuwún	手腕
write	sé	寫
write (a letter)	séseun	寫信
write down	sédài	寫低
written examination	bātsíh	筆試
wrong	cho	錯

X

X-ray	X-gwòng	X光
xerox	yíngyan	影印

Y

yacht	yàuhtéhng	遊艇
Yangtze River	Chèuhnggòng	長江
yard (3 feet)	máh	碼
yarn, wool	lāang	冷
yawn, yawning	dá haamlòuh	打喊露
year	nìhn	年
year after next	hauhnín, hauhnìhn	後年
year before last	chìhnnín, chìhnnìhn	前年
yell	ngaai	嗌
yellow (colour)	wòhngsīk, wòhng	黃色，黃
Yellow River	Wòhnghòh	黃河
yes	haih	係
yesterday	chàhmyaht, kàhmyaht	噚日，琴日
yet, but	daahnhaih	但係
you (pl.)	néihdeih	你哋
you (sing.)	néih	你
you're welcome	m̀sáihaakhei	唔駛客氣
young fellow	hauhsāangjái	後生仔
yourself	néihjihgéi	你自己

Z

zeal	yihtsìhng, yihtsàm	熱誠，熱心
zebra	bāanmáh	斑馬
zero	lìhng	零
zipper	lāailín	拉鍊

zoo	duhngmahtyùhn	動物園
zoology	duhngmahthohk	動物學

Part II

Specialized Glossaries,
with special Reference to Hong Kong.

(1) Where to go in Hong Kong

Names of Places	Deihkèui Méng	地區名
Hong Kong	Hèunggóng	香港
Aberdeen	Hèunggóngjái	香港仔
Causeway Bay	Tùhnglòhwàahn	銅鑼灣
Central District	Jùngwàahn	中環
Chai Wan	Chàaihwāan	柴灣
Happy Valley	Páaumáhdéi	跑馬地
Kennedy Town	Gīnnèihdeihsìhng	堅尼地城
Mid-Level	Bunsāankèui	半山區
North Point	Bākgok	北角
Quarry Bay	Jākyùhchùng	鰂魚涌
Sai Wan	Sāiwàahn	西環
Sai Wan Ho	Sāiwàanhó	西灣河
Sai Ying Pun	Sāiyìhngpùhn	西營盤
Shau Kei Wan	Sāaugēiwāan	筲箕灣
Shek O	Sehkngou	石澳
Sheung Wan	Seuhngwàahn	上環
Stanley	Chekchyúh	赤柱
Tai Hang	Daaihhāang	大坑
The Peak	Sāandéng	山頂
Victoria Peak	Chékèihsāandéng (sāandéng)	扯旗山頂 （山頂）
Wanchai	Wāanjái	灣仔
Wong Chuk Hang	Wòhngjūkhāang	黃竹坑
Kowloon	Gáulùhng	九龍
Cheung Sha Wan	Chèuhngsāwàahn	長沙灣
Choi Hung	Chóihùhng	彩虹
East Tsim Sha Tsui	Jīmdùng	尖東
Ho Man Tin	Hòhmàhntìhn	何文田

Hung Hom	Hùhngham	紅磡
Kowloon City	Gáulùhngsìhng	九龍城
Kowloon Tong	Gáulùhngtòhng	九龍塘
Kwun Tong	Gùntòhng	官塘
Lai Chi Kok	Laihjìgok	荔枝角
Lam Tin	Làahmtìhn	藍田
Lei Yue Mun	Léihyùhmùhn	鯉魚門
Mong Kok	Wohnggok	旺角
Ngau Tau Kok	Ngàuhtàuhgok	牛頭角
San Po Kong	Sànpòuhgòng	新蒲崗
Sham Shui Po	Sàmséuibóu	深水埗
Shek Kip Mei	Sehkgipméih	石硤尾
Tai Kok Tsui	Daaihgokjéui	大角咀
To Kwa Wan	Tóugwàwàahn	土瓜灣
Tse Wan Shan	Chìhwàhnsāan	慈雲山
Tsim Sha Tsui	Jìmsàjéui	尖沙咀
Wang Tau Hom	Wàahngtàuhham	橫頭磡
Wong Tai Sin	Wòhngdaaihsìn	黃大仙
Yau Ma Tei	Yàuhmàhdéi	油麻地
Yau Tong	Yàuhtòhng	油塘
Yau Yat Chuen	Yauhyātchyùn	又一村
New Territories	Sàngaai	新界
Castle Peak	Chìngsàan	青山
Fanling	Fánlèhng	粉嶺
Fo Tan	Fótaan	火炭
Kwai Chung	Kwàihchùng	葵涌
Lo Wu	Lòhwùh	羅湖
Lok Ma Chau	Lohkmáhjàu	落馬洲
Pearl Island	Lùhngjyūdóu	龍珠島
Sai Kung	Sàigung	西貢
Sha Tin	Sātìhn	沙田
Sheung Shui	Sheuhngséui	上水
Tai Po	Daaihbou	大埔
Tai Po Market	Daaihbouhèui	大埔墟
Tai Wai	Daaihwàih	大圍
Tsing Yi	Chìngyì	青衣

Tsuen Wan	Chyùhnwàan	荃灣
Tuen Mun	Tyùhnmùhn	屯門
Yuen Long	Yùhnlóhng	元朗

Beaches and Bays Góngwāan 港灣

Big Wave Bay	Daaihlohngwāan	大浪灣
Chek Lap Kok	Cheklaahpgok	赤鱲角
Clear Water Bay	Chìngséuiwāan	清水灣
Deep Water Bay	Sàmséuiwāan	深水灣
Discovery Bay	Yùhgíngwāan	愉景灣
	(Daaihbaahkwāan)	（大白灣）
Hau Hoi Wan	Hauhhóiwāan	后海灣
(Deep Bay)		
Junk Bay	Jèunggwànngou	將軍澳
Kowloon Bay	Gáulùhngwāan	九龍灣
Lei Yue Mun	Léihyùhmùhn	鯉魚門
Repulse Bay	Chínséuiwāan	淺水灣
Silver Mine Bay	Ngàhnkwongwāan	銀礦灣
Tai Long Wan	Daaihlohngwāan	大浪灣
Tolo Harbour	Toulouhgóng	吐露港
Victoria Harbour	Wàihdòleihngagóng	維多利亞港

Outlying Islands Lèihdóu 離島

Ap Lei Chau	Ngaapleihjàu	鴨脷洲
Cheung Chau	Chèuhngjàu	長洲
Hei Ling Chau	Héilìhngjàu	喜靈洲
Lamma Island	Nàahmngādóu	南丫島
Lantau Island	Daaihyùhsāan	大嶼山
Peng Chau	Pìhngjàu	坪洲
Po Toi Island	Pòuhtòihdóu	蒲台島

131

| Stonecutters Island | Ngóhnsyùhnjàu | 昂船洲 |

Country Parks	Gāauyéh Gùngyún	郊野公園
Aberdeen	Hèunggóngjái	香港仔
Cheung Sheung	Jèungsheuhng	嶂上
Chi Ma Wan	Jìmàhwāan	芝麻灣
Clear Water Bay	Chìngséuiwāan	清水灣
Hoi Ha	Hóihah	海下
Kei Ling Ha	Kéihléhnghah	企嶺下
Keung Shan	Gèungsàan	羌山
Kowloon Hill	Gáulùhngsāan	九龍山
Pokfulam	Bokfuhlàhm	薄扶林
Quarry Bay	Jākyùhchùng	鰂魚涌
Sai Kung	Sàigung	西貢
Sham Tseng	Sàmjéng	深井
Shek Pik	Sehkbīk	石壁
Shing Mun	Shìhngmùhn	城門
Tai Mei Tuk	Daaihméihdūk	大尾篤
Tai Po Kau	Daaihbougaau	大埔滘
Tai Lam Chung	Daaihláahmchùng	大欖涌
Tai Tam	Daaihtàahm	大潭
Tung Chung Au	Dùngchùngngaau	東涌坳
Twisk	Chyùhngám	荃錦

Reservoirs	Séuifu	水庫
Aberdeen Reservoir	Hèunggóngjái Séuitòhng	香港仔水塘
High Island Reservior	Maahnyìh Séuifu	萬宜水庫

Jubilee (Shing Mun) Reservoir	Sìhngmùhn Séuitòhng	城門水塘
Plover Cove Reservoir	SyùhnwāanTáahm-séuiwùh	船灣淡水湖
Pok Fu Lam Reservoir	Bokfuhlàhm Séuitòhng	薄扶林水塘
Shek Pik Reservoir	Sehkbīk Séuitòhng	石壁水塘
Tai Lam Chung Reservoir	Daaihláahmchùng Séuitòhng	大欖涌水塘
Tai Tam Reservoir	Daaihtàahm Séuitòhng	大潭水塘

(2) How to get there

Transportation	Gàautùng	交通
a chain collision	lìhnwàahn johngchè	連環撞車
Aberdeen Tunnel (Happy Valley -- Aberdeen)	Hèunggóngjái Seuihdouh	香港仔隧道
accelerator	yáumùhn, yàuhmùhn	油門
adjustable mirror	douhauhgeng	倒後鏡
Airport Tunnel	Gèichèuhng seuihdouh	機場隧道
Blake Pier	Bŭkgùng Máhtàuh	卜公碼頭
blow horn	gahmhōn, héungōn	撳安，響安
bright, high light	gòudàng	高燈
bus	bāsí	巴士
car fare	chèfai	車費
car park	tìhngchèchèuhng	停車場
Central Harbour Services Pier	Jùngwàahn Góngnoihsin Máhtàuh	中環港內線碼頭
common stored value ticket	tùngyuhng chyúhjihkpiu	通用儲值票
convenient	fòngbihn	方便
convertible	hòipùhngchè	開蓬車
Cross-Harbour Tunnel (Wan Chai -- Hung Hom)	Hóidái Seuihdouh	海底隧道
crowed	bīk	逼
dangerous driving	ngàihhím gasái	危險駕駛
dim, low light	dàidàng	低燈
don't have coins for the fare	móuh sáanngán	冇散銀
driving license	gasái jāpjiu, chèpàaih	駕駛執照，車牌

driving test	háau chè	考車
driving without license	mòuh pàaih gasái	無牌駕駛
economic class	gìngjaihaakwái	經濟客位
Edinburgh Place Terminal	Ngoidìngbóu Gwóngchèuhng Màhtàuh	愛丁保廣場碼頭
emergency stop	gángāp saatchè	緊急利車
franchise public light bus	jyūnsin síubā	專線小巴
garage	chèfòhng	車房
gas station	dihnyàuhjaahm	電油站
Get on the wrong bus	daap chochè	搭錯車
get stuck	pàaumàauh, pàaulàauh	拋錨
Hong Kong and Macau Ferry Terminal	Góng-Ngou Màhtàuh	港澳碼頭
Hong Kong and Yaumati Ferry	Yàuhmàhdéi Síulèuhn	油麻地小輪
Hong Kong International Airport (Kai Tak Airport)	Hèunggóng Gwokjai Gèichèuhng (Káidāk Gèichèuhng)	香港國際機場（啟德機場）
Hunghom Ferry Pier	Hùhngham Màhtàuh	紅磡碼頭
Hunghom Railway Station	Hùhngham Fóchè Júngjaahm	紅磡火車總站
hydrofoil	séuiyihksyùhn	水翼船
in a hurry	gón sìhgaan	趕時間
jalopy	lóuhyèhchè	老爺車
Kowloon - Canton Railway (Kowloon - Lo Wu, China border)	Gáu-Gwóng Titlouh	九廣鐵路

Lion Rock Tunnel (Waterloo Rd -- Shatin)	Sijisàan Seuihdouh	獅子山隧道
meter	māibīu	咪錶
minibus (Public light bus)	síubā	小巴
MTR -- Mass Transit Railway -- subway system	deihhah titlouh, deihtit	地下鐵路，地鐵
multi-storeyed garage	dòchàhng tihngchèchèuhng	多層停車場
no entry	bātjéun sáiyahp	不准駛入
no parking	bātjéun tihngchè	不准停車
no right(left)turn	bātjéun yauh(jó)jyun	不准右(左)轉
North Point Vehicle Ferry Pier	Bākgok Heichè Máhtàuh	北角汽車碼頭
North Point Ferry Pier	Bākgok Máhtàuh	北角碼頭
number plate	chèpàaih	車牌
Ocean Terminal	Hóiwahn Daaihhah	海運大廈
one way only	dāan-chìhng louh	單程路
Outlying Districts Services Pier	Jùngkèui Góngngoihsin Máhtàuh	中區港外線碼頭
overtaking, passing	pàhtàuh	扒頭
parking meter	hek gokjí lóuhfúgèi, tihngchè sàufaibīu	吃角子老虎機，停車收費錶
Peak Tram	Sàandéng laahmchè	山頂纜車
pier	máhtàuh	碼頭
plane	fèigèi	飛機
plane ticket	gèipiu	機票
Please let me off (telling the minibus driver)	yáuh lohk	有落

public coach	hòuhwàh bāsí	豪華巴士
public transpor- tation	gùngguhng gàautùng	公共交通
refuel	yahpyáu	入油
reverse	teuihauh	退後
roll backward	làuhhauh	溜後
safety first	ngònchyùhn daihyāt	安全第一
safety island	ngònchyùhn dóu	安全島
school bus (for children)	bóumóuhchè	保姆車
second-hand car	yihsáuchè	二手車
sport-car	páauchè	跑車
Star Ferry	Tìnsìng Síulèuhn	天星小輪
Star Ferry Pier (HK side)	Tìnsìng Máhtàuh	天星碼頭
Star Ferry Pier (Kowloon side)	Jìmsàjéui Máhtàuh	尖沙咀碼頭
student driver	hohksàhn	學神
subway station	deihtitjaahm	地鐵站
taxi	dīksí	的士
the car (engine) stops	séifó	死火
the tyre is leaking	lauh hei	漏氣
through train (Kowloon-Canton)	jihktùngchè	直通車
traffic control	gàautùng gúnjai	交通管制
traffic jam	sàkchè	塞車
traffic light	gàautùngdàng, hùhngluhkdàng	交通燈 紅綠燈
traffic signs	gàautùng bīuji	交通標誌
tram	dihnchè	電車
tunnel bus	seuihdouh bāsí	隧道巴士
turn indicator	jífài dàng	指揮燈
typhoon shelter	beihfùngtòhng	避風塘
use the turn indicator	dá jífàidàng	打指揮燈

| wind-shield wiper | séuibuht | 水撥 |
| zebra crossing, zebra stripes | bāanmáhsin | 斑馬線 |

MTR and KCR stations

| | Deihtit kahp Gáugwóng Titlouh Chèjaahm | 地鐵及九廣鐵路車站 |

Mass Transit Railway (MTR)	Deihhah Titlouh, deihtit	地下鐵路，地鐵
MTR stations	deihtit jaahm	地鐵站
Island Line :	Góngdóusin	港島線
Chai Wan	Chàaihwāan	柴灣
Heng Fa Chuen	Hahngfāchyùn	杏花村
Shaukeiwan	Sāaugèiwàan	筲箕灣
Sai Wan Ho	Sāiwàanhó	西灣河
Tai Koo	Taaigú	太古
Quarry Bay	Jākyùhchùng	鰂魚涌
North Point	Bākgok	北角
Fortress Hill	Paautòihsàan	炮台山
Tin Hau	Tìnhauh	天后
Causeway Bay	Tùhnglòhwàahn	銅鑼灣
Wan Chai	Wāanjái	灣仔
Admiralty	Gàmjùng	金鐘
Central	Jùngwàahn	中環
Sheung Wan	Seuhngwàahn	上環
interchange	jyunchèchyu	轉車處

Kwun Tong Line :	Gùntòhngsin	官塘線
Yaumati	Yàuhmàhdéi	油麻地
Mongkok	Wohnggok	旺角
Prince Edward	Taaijí	太子
Shek Kip Mei	Sehkgipméih	石硤尾
Kowloon Tong	Gáulùhngtòhng	九龍塘

Lok Fu	Lohkfu	樂富
Wong Tai Sin	Wòhngdaaihsīn	黃大仙
Diamond Hill	Jyunsehksàan	鑽石山
Choi Hung	Chóihùhng	彩虹
Kowloon Bay	Gáulùhngwāan	九龍灣
Ngau Tau Kok	Ngàuhtàuhgok	牛頭角
Kwun Tong	Gùntòhng	觀塘
Lam Tin	Làahmtìhn	藍田
Tsuen Wan Line :	Chyùhnwāansin	荃灣線
Central	Jùngwàahn	中環
Admiralty	Gàmjùng	金鐘
Tsim Sha Tsui	Jìmsàjéui	尖沙咀
Jordon	Jódēun	佐敦
Yaumati	Yàuhmàhdéi	油麻地
Mongkok	Wohnggok	旺角
Prince Edward	Taaijí	太子
Sham Shui Po	Sàmséuibóu	深水埗
Cheung Sha Wan	Chèuhngsāwàahn	長沙灣
Lai Chi Kok	Laihjìgok	荔枝角
Mei Foo	Méihfù	美孚
Lai King	Laihgíng	荔景
Kwai Fong	Kwàihfòng	葵芳
Kwai Hing	Kwàihhìng	葵興
Tai Wo Hau	Daaihwōháu	大窩口
Tsuen Wan	Chyùhnwāan	荃灣
Kowloon-Canton Railway (KCR)	Gáu Gwóng Titlouh	九廣鐵路
train station :	fóchèjaahm	火車站
Kowloon	Gáulùhng	九龍
Mong Kok	Wohnggok	旺角
Kowloon Tong	Gáulùhngtòhng	九龍塘
Tai Wai	Daaihwàaih	大圍
Sha Tin	Sàtìhn	沙田
Fo Tan	Fótaan	火炭

Racecourse	Máhchèuhng	馬場
University	Daaihhohk	大學
Tai Po Market	Daaihbou	大埔
Tai Wo	Taaiwòh	太和
Fan Ling	Fánléhng	粉嶺
Sheung Shui	Seuhngséui	上水
Lo Wu	Lòhwùh	羅湖

(3) What to do

Recreation and Sports	Yùhlohk kahp wahnduhng	娛樂及運動
academy awards	gàmjeunhgjéung	金像獎
admission ticket	yahpchèuhnggyun	入場券
adroit, agile	máhnjiht	敏捷
adversary, counterpart	deuisáu	對手
age limit	nìhnlìhng hahnjai	年齡限制
aggregate score	júngjikfàn	總績分
air bubble	chùnghei jeungmohk	充氣帳幕
all up betting	gwogwàan tàuhjyu	過關投注
all-around sportsman	chyùhnnàhng wahnduhngyùhn	全能運動員
all-events champion	chyùhnnàhng gungwàn	全能冠軍
all-star team	mìhngsìngdéui	明星隊
all-weather surface	chyùhntinhauh páaudouh	全天候跑道
Amah Rock	Mohngfùsàan	望夫山
amateur	yihpyùh wahnduhng-yùhn	業餘運動員
Amateur Sports Federation and Olympic Committee of HK	Hèunggóng Ngouwáiwúi	香港奧委會
ambidextrous	jóyauhsáu dòunàhngyuhng ge	左右手都能用嘅
announcement of results	sìhngjìk gùngbou	成績公佈
apparatus equipment	heihaaih	器械

apparel, costume, attire	fuhkjòng	服裝
appeal committee	juhngchòih wáiyùhnwúi	仲裁委員會
applause, cheer	hotchói	喝采
apprentice	ginjaahp kèhsì	見習騎師
aquaplaner	waahtséui wahnduhngyùhn	滑水運動員
archery	sehjin	射箭
arena	jyúchèuhng	主場
Art Festival	Ngaihseuhtjit	藝術節
artificial turf	yàhnjouh chóupèih	人造草皮
Asian Art Festival	Ngajàu Ngaihseuhtjit	亞洲藝術節
athlete, sports-man	wahnduhngyùhn	運動員
athletic meet	wahnduhngwúi	運動會
award	jéungbán	獎品
away ground	haakfòng choichèuhng	客方賽場
back stall	hauhjoh	後座
back stroke	buiwihng	背泳
badminton	yúhmòuhkàuh	羽毛球
ball games	kàuhleuih wahnduhng	球類運動
ball talk	kàuhgìng	球經
banish, foul out, chase out	faht chēutchèuhng	罰出場
banker	máhdáam	馬胆
bar	jáubà	酒巴
barbecue (B.B.Q.)	siuyéhsihk, yéhfówúi	燒嘢食,野火會
barred horses	tihngchoi máhpāt	停賽馬匹
baseball	páahngkàuh	棒球
basketball	làahmkàuh	籃球
beat, win	yèhng, sing	贏,勝
bench coach	làhmchèuhng gaaulihn	臨場教練
berth	yahpwàih	入圍
best actor (movie king)	yingdai	影帝

142

best actress (movie queen)	yínghauh	影后
betting	bokchói	博彩
betting centre	tàuhjyujaahm	投注站
betting pool	(tàuhjyu) chóichìh	（投注）彩池
betting ticket	bokchói chóipiu	博彩彩票
billiards	cheukkàuh	桌球
billiards parlour	cheukkàuhsàt	桌球室
black and white picture	hāakbaahk pín	黑白片
bleachers	louhtìn hontòih	露天看台
blinkers	ngáahnjaau	眼罩
body building exercise	gihnsànchòu	健身操
Bonus	dahkjéung	特獎
boo	hèusèng	嘘聲
book in advance	dehng wái	訂位
booking office	piufòhng	票房
bowling	bóulihngkàuh	保齡球
boxing	kyùhngìk wahnduhng	拳擊運動
break the record	pogéiluhk	破紀錄
break the world record	po saigaai géiluhk	破世界紀錄
breast stroke	wàsik	蛙式
bridge	kìuhpáai	橋牌
bring down, defeat, out perform	dábaaih	打敗
broad jump	tiuyúhn	跳遠
broad jump pit	sàchìh	沙池
bronze medal winner	gwaigwàn	季軍
butterfly stroke	wùhdihpsìk, dihpwìhng	蝴蝶式，蝶泳
calisthenics	yàuhyúhn táichòu	柔軟體操
call off	làhmsìh chéuisìu	臨時取消
call the score	bou fàn	報分

call the toss	jaahkngán dihng syùyèhng	擲銀定輸贏
canoe	duhkmuhkjàu	獨木舟
canoe polo	duhkmuhkjàu séuikàuh	獨木舟水球
Canoeing	duhkmuhkjàu wahnduhng	獨木舟運動
Cantonese picture	yuhtyúh pín	粵語片
capacity crowd, full house, sold out	múhnjoh	滿座
captain	deuihjéung	隊長
carry a game	sing yātguhk	勝一局
cartoon	kàtùng pín	卡通片
catamaran vessel	sèungtái syùhn	雙體船
chalk up / create a record	chong géiluhk	創紀錄
champion, gold medallist	gungwàn	冠軍
championship match	gámbìuchoi	錦標賽
championship race (horse race)	gámbìuchoi	錦標賽
change of courts/ of ends/ of goals	gàauwuhn chèuhngdeih	交換場地
cheer-team, cheering-section	làlàdéui	啦啦隊
chess	gwokjai jeuhngkéi	國際象棋
Chinese chess	Jeuhngkéi	象棋
Chinese kung-fu	Jùnggwok gùngfù	中國功夫
choice of ends	syúnjaahk chèuhngdeih	選擇場地
chronograph	míuhbìu	秒錶
clash, play, contend against	deuijahn	對陣
closing ceremony	baimohk yìhsìk	閉幕儀式

closing date for entries	jihtjí boumèng yahtkèih	截止報名日期
coach	gaaulihn	教練
coast home, walk-away, easy victory	hingyih chéuising	輕易取勝
combinations	gwogwàan jóuhahp	過關組合
coming attraction	yuhgoupín	預告片
coming soon	bātyaht fongyíng	不日放映
competition season	gihngchoi gwaijit	競賽季節
competitor, contestant	chàamchoijé	參賽者
conduct of draw	chàuchìm	抽簽
consolation	ngònwaijéung	安慰獎
consolation tournament	ngònwaichoi	安慰賽
contest	béichoi	比賽
Country Club	Hèungchyùn Kèuilohkbouh	鄉村俱樂部
Country Park	Gàauyéh Gùngyún	郊野公園
covered playground	yáuhgoi chòuchèuhng	有蓋操場
Cowboy show	ngáuhjái pín	牛仔片
cricket	báankàuh	板球
cross betting	sèungbin tàuhjyu	雙邊投注
cycle racing	dàanchè béicho'	單車比賽
deadlock	gèungguhk	僵局
default, withdraw	heikyùhn	棄權
defend one's title	waihmíhn	衛冕
defending team/ side	fòhngsáudéui	防守隊
detective film	jìngtaam pín	偵探片
discus throw	jaahk titbéng	擲鐵餅
dispute a title	jàngdyuht gwungwàn	爭奪冠軍
disqualify	tòuhtaai	淘汰

disqualify, debar	chéuisiu béichoijigaak	取消比賽資格
distrubution of awards	bàanfaat jéungbán	頒發獎品
diver	chìhmséuiyùhn	潛水員
dividend	chóigàm	彩金
diving board	tiubáan	跳板
division	(siu) jóu	（小）組
documentary film	géiluhk pín	紀錄片
dominate a game	jim ngaatdóusing yàusai	占壓倒性優勢
dope test	sáiyuhng hìngfáhnjài gimchàh	使用興奮劑檢查
double elimination	sèung tòuhtaaijai	雙淘汰制
doubles	séungdá, sèungyàhnchoi	雙打，雙人賽
dragon-boat racing	lùhngjàu gihngchoi, pàhlùhngsyùhn	龍舟競賽，扒龍船
draw	dásìhng pìhngguhk	打成平局
dress circle	dahkdáng	特等
dressing/ changing room	gàngyisàt	更衣室
drill, training, exercise	chòulihn	操練
drop out	jùngtòuh teuichēut béichoi	中途退出比賽
edge, nose ahead	sáauwàih líhngsìn	稍為領先
elimination style contest	tòuhtaaichoi	淘汰賽
equalize a record	pìhnggéiluhk	平紀錄
event	béichoi hohngmuhk	比賽項目
ex-champion	chìhngwùngwàn	前冠軍
exchange of pennants	gàauwùhn déuikèih	交換隊旗
exhibition match/ competition	bíuyíngchoi	表演賽

exotic bets	sànfúntàuhjyu fòngsìk	新款投注方式
fair play trophy	fùnggaakjéung	風格獎
fans	yúngdán	擁躉
featherweight (boxing)	yuhleuhngkāp	羽量級
fencing	gimgīk	劍擊
fiction film, literary film	màhnngaih pín	文藝片
field sports	yéhngoih wahnduhng	野外運動
fighting picture	dádau pín	打鬥片
figure skating	fāsìk làuhbìng	花式溜冰
final contest, finals, final round	kyutchoi	決賽
finish, finish line	jùngdím	終點
first contest	chòchoi	初賽
First prize payout	tàuhjéung jéunggàm	頭獎獎金
first run theatre	sáulèuhn heiyún	首輪戲院
fishing	diuyú	釣魚
fitness test	sàntáijātsou chàakyihm	身體質素測驗
fitness trail	gihnsànging	健身徑
flash card	(chòihpunyuhngge) sihfànpáai	（裁判用嘅）示分牌
fluke	hìuhahng chéuising	僥倖取勝
foil fencing	sàiyèuhng gimgīk	西洋劍擊
foreign picture	sài pín	西片
formula	tàuhjyu fòngsìk	投注方式
free / complementary ticket	jahnggyuhn	贈券
free fight and kick boxing	jihyàuhbokgīk	自由博擊
free style	jihyàuhsìk	自由式
friendly match	yàuhyìhchoi	友誼賽

front stall	chìhnjoh	前座
full house	múhnjoh	滿座
gala premiere	yàusìn hinyíng	優先獻映
game	béichoi	比賽
game (M)	guhk	局
garrison finish, pull out of the fire	fáan baaih wàih sing	反敗爲勝
give a prize	bàanjéung	頒獎
go, weichi	wàihkéi	圍棋
goal net	lùhngmùhn	龍門
goalless draw	lihng béi lihng, pìhngguhk	零比零，平局
goggles	wuhngáahnjaau	護眼罩
golf	gòyíhfùkàuh	高爾夫球
golf course	gòyíhfùkàuhchèuhng	高爾夫球場
goose egg, horse-collar	lìhngfàn	零分
grand slam, sweep	wohk chyùhnsing	獲全勝
grandstand (covered)	(yáuhgoi) hontòih	（有蓋）看台
great!	hóuyéh!	好嘢！
gymnasium	gihnsànsàt	健身室
gymnastics	táichòu	體操
handball	sáukàuh	手球
have full power and discretion	chyùhnkyùhn chyúléih	全權處理
health club	gihnhòng jùngsàm	健康中心
heated swimming pool	lyúhnséui wìhngchìh	暖水泳池
high jump	tiugòu	跳高
highest total pinfall (bowling)	jeuigòu jīkfàn	最高積分
hiring charge	jòuyuhng fai	租用費
hockey	kūkgwankàuh	曲棍球
hold the record	bóuchìh géiluhk	保持紀錄

home team /side	jyúdéui	主隊
Hong Kong Football Association	Hèunggóng Jūkkàuh Júngwúi	香港足球總會
Hong Kong Coliseum	(Hèunggóng) Hùhngham Táiyuhkgún	（香港）紅磡 體育館
Hong Kong Stadium	(Jingfú) Daaihkàuhchèuhng	（政府）大球 場
horror film	húngbou pín	恐怖片
horse racing	choimáh, páaumáh	賽馬，跑車
host country	jyúbaahngwok	主辦國
hurdle	tiulàahn	跳欄
hurry up, faster	faaidí, gàyáu	快的，加油
ice hockey	bìngseuhng kūkgwankàuh	冰上曲棍球
ice sports	bìngseuhng wahnduhng	冰上運動
in good form, in top shape	johngtaai hóu	狀態好
in the saddle	chaatkèh	策騎
individual competition	goyàhn béichoi	個人比賽
indoor competition	sātnoih béichoi	室內比賽
indoor games hall	sātnoih táiyuhkgún	室內體育館
indoor sports	sātnoih wahnduhng	室內運動場
interest club / group	hingcheui síujóu	興趣小組
interschool competition	haauhjai béichoi	校際比賽
interval, intermission	yàusìk	休息
invitation tournament	yiuchíngchoi	邀請賽
javelin throwing	bìuchèung	標槍
jockey	kèhsì	騎師
jogging	wùhnbouhpáau, páaubouh	緩步跑，跑步

English	Cantonese	Chinese
Jubilee Sports Centre	Ngàhnhèi Táiyuhk Jùngsàm	銀禧體育中心
judo	yàuhdouh	柔道
jump the gun	tàubouh	偷步
Kam Tin Walled Village	Gámtìhnwàih	錦田圍
karate	hùngsáudouh	空手道
keep fit	bóuchìh sàntáigihnhòng	保持身體健康
keeping time	gaisìh	計時
Kendo	gimdouh	劍道
knockout / qualifying match	tòuhtaaichoi	淘汰賽
Lai Chi Kok Amusement Park	Laihyún	荔園
lap	yāthyùn	一圈
Lau Fau Shan	Làuhfàuhsàan	流浮山
lawn bowls	chóudéigwánkàuh	草地滾球
league matches	lyùhnchoi	聯賽
life-guard	gausàngyùhn	救生員
lightweight (boxing)	hìngleuhngkāp	輕量級
line-up	jahnyùhng	陣容
linesman	sisinyùhn	司線員
load	yahpjaahp	入閘
locker room	chityáuh yìmahtsèung ge gàngyisàt	設有衣物箱嘅更衣室
lodge seat	chiudáng	超等
Lok Ma Chau	Lohkmáhjàu	落馬洲
lop-sided, one-sided	yātbìndóu	一邊倒
lose, bow, concede	syù	輸
manager, maestro	líhngdéui	領隊
Mandarin picture	gwokyúh pín	國語片
Marathon race	Máhlàaichùhng páau	馬拉松跑
Mark Six	Luhkhahpchói	六合彩

150

match	choisih	賽事
member's enclo- sure (Jockey Club)	wúiyùhnpàahng	會員棚
men's team	nàahmjí jóu	男子組
meter	gùngchek	公尺
mid-night show	nǵhyehchèuhng	午夜場
midfield player	jùngchèuhng kàuhyùhn	中場球員
mini-soccer pitch	siuyìhng jùkkàuhchèuhng	小型足球場
mixed team	nàahmnéuih wahnhahpdéui	男女混合隊
morning show	jóu chèuhng	早場
mountaineering	pàhsàan wahnduhng	爬山運動
movie	dihnyíng	電影
movie star	(dihnyíng) mìhngsìng	（電影）明星
music director	yàmngohk júnggàam	音樂總監
neck and neck	bātsèungseuhnghah	不相上下
new record	sàn géiluhk	新紀錄
next change	hahkèih fongyíng	下期放映
nick, nose out	hímsing	險勝
novice, new- comer, beginner	sànsáu	新手
odds	pùihléut	賠率
off course betting	ngoihwàih tàuhjyu	外圍投注
off form, out of shape	sàtsèuhng	失常
old warhorse	lóuhjeung	老將
Olympic Games	Ngouwahnwúi, Saiwahnwúi	奧運會，世運 會
on course betting	yìhngchèuhng tàuhjyu	現場投注
open competition/ tournament	gùnghòichoi	公開賽
open playground	louhtìn chòuchèuhng	露天操場
open showers	louhtìn fàsá	露天花洒

open-air competition	louhtìn béichoi	露天比賽
Oscar	Ngousìkà gàmjeuhngjéung	奧斯卡金像獎
owner of a horse	máhjyú	馬主
panel of judges	pìhngsyúntyùhn	評選團
parade ring (for horses)	sāhyùn	沙圈
parallel bars	sèunggong	雙槓
pari-mutuel	chóichìh	彩池
pay out	paaichoi	派彩
pelota, jai alai	wùihlihkkàuh	回力球
performer	bíuyínjé	表演者
physique	táigaak	體格
ping-pong ball (table tennis)	bìngbàmbò	乒乓波
ping-pong paddle	bōpáak	波拍
ping-pong table	bìngbàmbò tói	乒乓波枱
play rough	duhngjok chòuyéh	動作粗野
playing rules	béichoi kwàilaih	比賽規例
pole vault jump	chìhgòntiu	持竿跳
polo	máhkàuh	馬球
posture, pose, carriage, form	jìsai	姿勢
preliminary round	yuhchoi	預賽
press box	geijéjihk	記者席
preview	wàtàuh	畫頭
prize-awarding, prize-giving ceremony	bàanjéung dínláih	頒獎典禮
professional, pro	jīkyihp wahnduhng-yùhn	職業運動員
public swimming pool	gùngjung wihngchìh	公衆泳池
pull up, catch up	yìhngtàuhgónséuhng	迎頭趕上
punter	tàuhjyujé	投注者

152

qualifying round	yànbihtchoi	甄別賽
Quantet	seichùhngchói	四重彩
Queen Elizabeth Stadium	Yìleihsàbaak Táiyuhkgún	伊利沙白體育館
Quinella	lìhnyèhng	連贏
race number (horse race)	chèuhngchi	場次
racecourse	máhchèuhng, choimáhchèuhng	馬場，賽馬場
raft	fàuhtòih	浮台
receive a prize	lìhngjéung	領獎
record breaking	po géiluhk	破紀錄
recreational programme	hònglohk jitmuhk	康樂節目
referee, umpire	kàuhjing	球證
registered retainer	sauhping kèhsì	受聘騎師
regular show	jing chèuhng	正場
reigning champion	búngaai gungwàn	本屆冠軍
relay	jiplihkchoi	接力賽
relegation	gonkàp	降級
repose, rest period	yàusìk sìhgaan	休息時間
reverse, substitute	hauhbeih kàuhyùhn	後備球員
roller skating	gwánjuhk làuhbìng	滾軸溜冰
round robin, all play with all	chèuhnwàahnchoi	循環賽
rowing, boating	pàhtéhng	扒艇
Royal Hong Kong Jockey Club	Hèunggóng Wòhnggà Choimáhwúi, Máhwúi	香港皇家賽馬會，馬會
rubber game	kyutsingguhk	決勝局
rugby	láamkàuh	欖球
runner-up, silver medallist	ngagwàn	亞軍

153

rush seat	m̀deuihòuhge gùnjungjihk	唔對號旣公衆席
sailing	fùngfàahn wahnduhng	風帆運動
sauna	jìnghei yuhksāt	蒸氣浴室
science fiction movie	fòwaahn pín	科幻片
score	dākfan	得分
scoreboard	geifānpáai	記分牌
scorekeeper, socer	geifànyùhn	記分員
second run theatre	yihlèuhn heiyún	二輪影院
second-rated	yihlàuhge	二流旣
see-saw game	làaigeujin	拉鋸戰
seeded player	júngji syúnsáu	種子選手
select	syúnbaht	選拔
semi-final	jéunkyutchoi	準決賽
shooting	sehgìk	射擊
shot putting	tèuiyùhnkàuh	推鉛球
shower facilities	chùngsàn chitbeih	冲身設備
side stroke	jākwìhng	側泳
singles	dàandá, dàanyàhnchoi	單打，單人賽
Six Up	Luhkwàahnchói	六環彩
skating	làuhbìng	溜冰
skating rink	làuhbìngchèuhng	溜冰場
skiing	waahtsyut	滑雪
skittles	gwánkàuh	滾球
snooker, billiards	tóibò, cheukkàuh	枱波，桌球
soccer, football	jūkkàuh	足球
softball	lèuihkàuh	壘球
solar-heated changing room	taaiyèuhngnàhng faatyiht gàngyìsàt	太陽能發熱更衣室
spectator stand	gùnjung hontòih	觀衆看台
spectators	gùnjung	觀衆
sports gear, sporting goods	táiyuhk yuhngbán	體育用品

154

sports journa- list, sports- writer	táiyuhk geijé	體育記者
sports world / circles	táiyuhkgaai	體育界
sportsmanship	táiyuhk jìngsàhn	體育精神
sprinter	dyúnpáaugà	短跑家
spy show	dahkmouh pín	特務片
squash	bìkkàuh	壁球
stage manage	móuhtòih gìngléih	舞台經理
standard pool	póutùng chóichìh	普通彩池
starter	chēutchoimáhpàt	出賽馬匹
starting pistol	seunhouhchèung	信號槍
starting point	héidím	起點
storeroom	chyúhmahtsāt	儲物室
substitution	taibou kàuhyúhn	替補球員
surf ahead, take a large lead	yìuhyìuh lìhngsìn	遙遙領先
swim	yàuhséui	游水
swimming gala	séuiwahnwúi	水運會
swimming suit	wihngyì yàuhséuisàam	泳衣，游水衫
swimming trunks	wihngfú, yàuhséuifu	泳褲，游泳褲
swords-man fighting movie	móuhhahp pín	武俠片
synchronised swimming	wáhnleuhtwìhng	韻律泳
synopsis	heikíu	戲橋
table tennis	bìngbàmbò	乒乓波
Taekwondo	Tòihkyùhndouh	跆拳道
Tai-chi (shadow Boxing)	Taaigihk(kyùhn)	太極（拳）
teacher-training pool	fanlihngchìh	訓練池
team / squad	deuihngh	隊伍
technicolor movie	chóisìk pín	彩色片

telebet (tele-phone betting)	dihnwá tàuhjyu	電話投注
third-string	sàamlàuhge	三流既
ticket taker	sàupiuyùhn	收票員
tie score	jĭkfàn sèungtùhng	積分相同
Tierce	Sàamchùhngchói	三重彩
time keeper	gaisìhyùhn	計時員
time out	jaahmtìhng	暫停
time up, gun time, final whistle	yùhnchèuhng	完場
to scalp	cháau fèi	炒飛
top-class, top-flight, top-notch	yàtlàuhge	一流既
toss, toss-up	jaahkngán kyutdihng	擲銀決定
tournament schedule	béichoi sìhgaanbíu	比賽時間表
track	páaudouh	跑道
trackwork, track gallop	sàhnchòu	晨操
trainer	lihnmáhsì	練馬師
trampoline	daahnchòhng	彈床
Treble	Sàambóu	三寶
tug-of-war	bahthòh, chédaaihlaahm	拔河，扯大纜
turnstile	jyunsàan	轉柵
TV film	dihnsih pín	電視片
TV star	dihnsih mìhngsìng	電視明星
up-and-coming star	hauhhéijìsau	後起之秀
usher	daaiwái	帶位
variety show	gòmóuh pín	歌舞片
velodrome	wúnyìhng dàanchèchèuhng	碗形單車場
versus	deui	對

vision display screen	yìhnggwòngmohk	營光幕
visiting team	haakdéui	客隊
volleyball	pàaihkàuh	排球
walkathon	bouhhàhng wahnduhng	步行運動
warming up / loosening up exercise	yihtsàn wahnduhng	熱身途動
water skiing	waahtséui	滑水
water/ aquatic sports, aquatics	séuiseuhng wahnduhng	水上運動
waterpolo	séuikàuh	水球
wave-surfing	chùnglohng wahnduhng	衝浪運動
weightlifting	géuichúhng	舉重
Western picture	sàibouh pin	西部片
win (horse race)	duhkyèhng	獨贏
win favourite	duhkyèhng daaihyihtmún	獨贏大熱門
windsurfing	waahtlohng fùngfàahn	滑浪風帆
withdrawal	teuichèut	退出
women's team	néuihjí jóu	女子組
wrestling	sèutgok	摔角
Yacht Club	Yàuhtéhngwúi	遊艇會
Yoga	Yùhgà	瑜迦

Museums	Bokmahtgún	博物館
Lei Cheng Uk Museum	Léihchehngngūk Bokmahtgún	李鄭屋博物館
Museum of Art	Hèunggóng Ngaihseuhtgún	香港藝術館
Museum of History	Hèunggóng Bokmahtgún	香港博物館
Museum of Tea Ware	Chàhgeuih Màhnmahtgún	茶具文物館
Space Museum	Taaihùnggún	太空館

157

Public Amenities	Gùngguhng Màhnyùhchitsì	公共文娛設施
Academic Community Hall	Daaihjyùn Wúitòhng	大專會堂
Arts Center	Ngaihseuht Jùngsàm	藝術中心
City Hall	Daaihwuihtòhng	大會堂
City Hall Concert Hall	Daaihwuihtòhng Yàmngohktèng	大會堂音樂廳
City Hall Theatre	Daaihwuihtòhng Kehkyún	大會堂劇院
Hong Kong Academy for Performing Arts	Hèunggóng Yínngaih Hohkyún	香港演藝學院
HongKong Coliseum	Hùhngham Táiyuhkgún	紅勵體育館
Ko Shan Theatre	Gòusàan Kehkchèuhng	高山劇場
Queen Elizabeth Stadium	Yìleihsàbaak Táiyuhkgún	伊利沙白體育館
Tuen Wan Town Hall	Chyùhnwàan Daaihwuihtòhng	荃灣大會堂
Yuen Long Town Hall	Yùhnlóhng Daaihwuihtòhng	元朗大會堂

Fine Arts	Ngaihseuht	藝術
City Contemporary Dance company	Sìhngsíh Dòngdoih Móuhdouhtyùhn	城市當代舞蹈團
Hong Kong Children's Choir	Hèunggóng Yìhtùhng Hahpcheungtyùhn	香港兒童合唱團
Hong Kong Chinese Orchestra	Hèunggóng Jùngngohktyùhn	香港中樂團
Hong Kong Dance Company	Hèunggóng Móuhdouhtyùhn	香港舞蹈團
Hong Kong Philharmonic Orchestra	Hèunggóng Gúnyìhnngohktyùhn	香港管弦樂團

| Hong Kong Repertory Theatre | Hèunggóng Wákehktyùhn | 香港話劇團 |
| Hong Kong Youth Theatre Company | Hèunggóng Chìngnihn Kehktyùhn | 香港青年劇團 |

Places of Interest   Hóu heuichyu   好去處

Chater Garden	Jèdá Gùngyún	遮打公園
floating seafood restaurant	hóisìnfóng	海鮮舫
Happy Valley Racecourse	Faaiwuhtgūk Máhchèuhng	快活谷，馬場
Hong Kong Park	Hèunggóng gùngyún	香港公園
Jade Market	yuhkhei sìhchèuhng	玉器市場
Lady's Market	Néuihyángàai	女人街
Ocean Park	Hóiyèuhng Gùngyún	海洋公園
Poor Man's Night Club	Pìhngmàhn Yehjúngwúi	平民夜總會
Sha Tin Racecourse	Sàtìhn Máhchèuhng	沙田馬場
Statue Square	Wòhnghauhjeuhng Gwóngchèuhng	皇后像廣場
Sung Dynasty Village	Sungsìhng	宋城
Tiger Balm Gardens	Fúpaau bihtseuih	虎豹別墅
Victoria Park	Waihdòleihnga Gùngyún	維多利亞公園
Water World	Séuiseuhng Lohkyùhn	水上樂園
Zoological & Botanical Gardens	Bìngtàuh Fāyún, Duhngjihkmaht Gùngyún	兵頭花園，動植物公園

Cinemas	heiyún	戲院
Columbia Classics	Sànwá	新華
Empress	Hóisìng	凱聲
Golden Harvest	Gàwòh	嘉禾
Harbour City Cinemas	Hóisìhng	海城
Imperial	Gìngdòu	京都
Isis	Sàndòu	新都
Jade	Féicheui	翡翠
King's	Yùhlohk	娛樂
Lee	Leihmóuhtòih	利舞台
Liberty	Faailohk	快樂
London	Lèuhndèun	倫敦
M2	Sàndaaihwàh	新大華
Majestic	Daaihwàh	大華
Nan Yang	Nàahmyéung	南洋
Ocean	Hóiwahn	海運
Palace	Bìklaihgùng	碧麗宮
Park	Baaklohk	百樂
Pearl	Mìhngjyù	明珠
President	Júngtúng	總統
Queen's	Wòhnghauh	皇后
Rex	Màhnwah	文華
Royal	Laihsìng	麗聲
State	Wòhngdòu	皇都
UA 6	UA Luhk	UA6
Washington	Wàhsìhngdeuhn	華盛頓

Chinese Musical Instruments	Jùnggwok ngohkhei	中國樂器
Bass gehu	daiyàm gaakwú	低音革胡
Daruan	daaihyún	大阮
Di	dék	笛

160

Erhu	yihwú	二胡
Gaohu	gòuwú	高胡
Gehu	gaakwú	革胡
Guan	gún	管
Guzheng	gújàng	古箏
Liuqin	láuhyihpkàhm	柳葉琴
Percussion	hàaugìk ngohkhei	敲擊樂器
Pipa	pèihpá	琵琶
Sanzian	sàamyìhn	三弦
Sheng	sāng	笙
Suona	sāaunahp	嗩吶
Yangqin	yèuhngkàhm	洋琴
Zhonghu	jùngwú	中胡
Zhongruan	jùngyún	中阮

(4) What to eat and drink

Food	seikbán	食品
appetizer	tàuhpún	頭盆
bacon	yinyuhk	煙肉
bean curd	dauhfu	豆腐
beef	ngàuhyuhk	牛肉
beverage	yámbán	飲品
bird's nest	yinwò	燕窩
bread	mihnbàau	麵飽
butter	ngàuhyàuh	牛油
cake	daahngòu	蛋糕
candy	tòng	糖
catchup (ketchup)	kéjàp	茄汁
cheese	jisi, chìsí	芝士
chestnut	leuhtjí	栗子
Chinese sausage	laahpchéung	臘腸
coldmeat platter	pìngpún	拼盆
congee, rice gruel	jùk	粥
cookies	kūkkèihbéng	曲奇餅
cornflakes	sūkmáihpín	粟米片
cube sugar	fòngtòhng	方糖
curry	galēi	咖喱
date	jóu	棗
dessert	tìhmbán	甜品
dimsum	dímsàm	點心
egg (preserved)	pèihdáan	皮蛋
eggwhite	dáanbáak	蛋白
fish	yú	魚
French fries	syùhtíu	薯條
frog	tìhngài	田鷄
ham	fótéui	火腿

162

hamburger	honbóubàau	漢堡包
hot dog	yihtgáu	熱狗
ingredients	yuhngliu	用料
instant noodle	gùngjáimihn, jiksihkmihn	公仔麵，即食麵
jam	gwójim	果占
lamb chop	yèuhngpá	羊扒
macaroni	tùngsàmfán	通心粉
main course	jyúchoi	主菜
milk	ngàuhnáaih	牛奶
mungbean vermicelli	fánsi	粉絲
noodle	mihn	麵
oatmeal	mahkpèih	麥皮
Peking duck	Bākgìngngáap	北京鴨
pie	pài	批
pigeon	yúhgaap	乳鴿
pizza	yidaaihleih bohkbéng	意大利薄餅
popsicle	syuttíu	雪條
pork chop	jyùpá	猪扒
pork rib	pàaihgwàt	排骨
pudding	boudīn	布甸
rice (cooked)	faahn	飯
rice gruel	lāanglóujùk, hèifaahn	冷佬粥，稀飯
rice-noodle	máihfán	米粉
roast duck	siùngaap	燒鴨
roast suckling pig	yúhjyù	乳猪
salad	sàléut	沙律
salad dressing	sàléutjeung	沙律醬
salt	yìhm	鹽
salty egg (preserved)	hàahmdáan	咸蛋
sandwich	sàammàhnjih	三文治
sausage	hèungchéung	香腸

163

seafood	hóisìn	海鮮
seasonings	tiuhmeihbán	調味品
shark's fin soup	yùhchi	魚翅
soup (thick)	gàng	羹
soup (thin)	tòng	湯
soy sauce	sihyàuh	豉油
steak	ngàuhpá	牛扒
steamed chicken	baahkchitgài	白切鶏
sugar	tòhng	糖
tomato sauce	fàankéjeung	蕃茄醬
veal cutlet	ngàuhjáiyuhk	牛仔肉
vinegar	chou	醋
walnut	hahptòuh	合桃
won-ton noodle	wàhntànmihn	雲吞麵
wonton	wàhntàn	雲吞
yogurt	syùnngàuhnáaih	酸牛奶

Basic Seasonings and Ingredients for Chinese Cooking	Jùngchoi tiuhmeihbán kahp yuhnglíu	中菜調味品及用料
Chinese rose wine	mùihgwailouh	玫瑰露
chilli sauce	laahtjiujeung	辣椒醬
chilli oil	laahtjiuyàuh	辣椒油
mustard paste	gaailaaht	芥辣
curry powder	galèifán	咖喱粉
red vinegar	jitchou	浙醋
scallops (dried)	gonyiuhchyúh	乾瑤柱
dried shrimps	hàmáih	蝦米
dried mushroom	dùnggù	冬菇
straw mushroom	chóuhgù	草菇
Jew's ear mushroom	wàhnyíh *cloud ears*	雲耳
sesame (black)	hàakjìmàh	黑芝麻

164

sesame (white)	baahkjìmàh	白芝麻
dates (red)	hùhngjóu	紅棗
dates (preserved honey)	mahtjóu	蜜棗
dried tangerine peel	gwópèih	果皮
pepper	wùhjìufán	胡椒粉
soysauce (light colour)	sàangchàu	生抽
soysauce (dark colour)	lóuhchàu	老抽
ginger	gèung	薑
green onion	chùng	葱
sugar	tòhng	糖
salt	yìhm	鹽
oil	yàuh	油
oyster sauce	hòuhyàuh	蠔油
sesame oil	màhyàuh	麻油
sesame sauce	jìmàhjeung	芝麻醬
fermented black beans	dauhsih	豆豉
fermented soybean paste	mihnsí	麵豉
Chinese Wine (shaohsing)	siuhhingjáu	紹興酒
triple distilled Chinese wine	sàamjìngjáu	三蒸酒

Cantonese Dishes	Gwóngdùng choi/ Yuht choi	廣東菜/粵菜
<u>Cold dish</u>	Láahngpún	冷盤
assorted barbecued meats	sìuméipìngpún	燒味拼盆
barbecued pork	chàsìu	叉燒

165

roasted goose	sīungó	燒鵝
roasted pork	sīuyuhk	燒肉
roasted spare-ribs	sīupàaihgwàt	燒排骨
soy sauce chicken	sihyàuhgài	豉油鷄
Soup	Tòng	湯
diced winter melon with mixed meats and seafood soup	jaahpgámdùnggwànāp- tòng	雜錦冬瓜粒湯
doubled boiled whole winter melon soup	dùnggwàjùng	冬瓜盅
minced beef and egg white soup	sàiwùhngàuhyuhkgàng	西湖牛肉羹
shark's fin soup with shredded chicken	gàisìchi	鷄絲翅
shredded duck meat with conpoy soup	gònyìuhchyúh ngaapsì gàng	乾瑤柱鴨絲羹
snake soup (in winter only)	sèhgàng	蛇羹
sweet corn with carb meat (or: minced chicken) soup	háaihyuhk/gàiyùhng- sùkméihgàng	蟹肉/鷄蓉粟米羹
Poultry	Gàingaap	雞鴨
deep-fried duckling with mashed taro	làihyùhng hèungsòu- ngaap	荔蓉香酥鴨
diced chicken with walnuts/ cashew nuts	hahptòuh/yìugwó gàidìng	合桃/腰果鷄丁
fried chicken	jajìgài	炸子鷄
pan-fried lemon duck/chicken	lìhngmùng ngaap/gài	檸檬鴨/鷄

roasted pigeon	sìuyúhgaap	燒乳鴿
Beef & Pork	yuhk	肉
deep-fried salt & pepper spare-ribs	jiuyìhm pàaihgwàt	椒鹽排骨
stir-fried sliced fillet of beef in oyster sauce	hòuhyàuh ngàuhyuhk	蠔油牛肉
sweet & sour pork	gùlòuyuhk	咕嚕肉
sweet & sour spare-ribs	sàangcháau pàaihgwàt	生炒排骨
Seafood	Hóisìn	海鮮
baked (fried) crab in ginger & onion sauce	gēungchùng guhkháaih	薑葱焗蟹
baked (fried) crab/lobster in black bean & chilli sauce	sihjìu guhkháaih/ lùhnghà	豉椒焗蟹/ 龍蝦
deep-fried crab claws	ja yeuhngháaihkìhm	炸釀蟹鉗
deep-fried salt & pepper squid	jiuyìhm sìnyáu	椒鹽鮮魷
fried prawns with garlic sauce	syunyùhnghà	蒜蓉蝦
fried prawns with salt, pepper & chilli	jiuyìhmhà	椒鹽蝦
poached shrimps (boiled shrimps)	baahkcheukhà	白灼蝦
sauteed broccoli with scallop	sàilàahnfà cháau daaijí	西蘭花炒帶子
steamed bean-curd stuffed with minced shrimp	baakfā jìngyeuhng dauhfuh	百花蒸釀豆腐

167

steamed fish in salted-bean sauce	sihjāp jìngyú	豉汁蒸魚
steamed garoupa	chìngjìngsehkbāan	清蒸石斑
Vegetable	Sōchoi	蔬菜
sauteed broccoli	cháau sàilàahnfā	炒西蘭花
sauteed chinese flowering vegetable	cháauchoisàm	炒菜心
sauteed chinese kale	cháau gaailáan	炒芥蘭
sauteed fresh asparagus	cháau sìnlouhséun	炒鮮露筍
sauteed fresh mushroom with crabmeat	háaihyuhk pàh sìngù	蟹肉扒鮮菇
sauteed pea-shoots with crabmeat	háaihyuhk pàh dauhmìuh	蟹肉扒豆苗
Desserts	Tìhmbán	甜品
almond soup	hahngyàhn wú	杏仁糊
honey dew melon sago soup with coconut juice	mahtgwà sàimáihlouh	蜜瓜西米露
red bean soup	hùhngdáu sà	紅豆沙

Chinese Tea	Jùnggwokchàh	中國茶
Chrysanthemum	Hòhngūk	杭菊
Jasmine Tea	Hèungpín	香片
Lok-on	Luhkngòn	六安
Lung-Ching	Lùhngjéng	龍井
Pu-erh	bóuléi	普洱
Pu-erh + Chrysanthemum	Gūkbóu	菊普

Shou-mei	Sauhméi	壽眉
Shui-hsien	Séuisìn	水仙
Tikuanyin	Titgùnyàm	鐵觀音 *very bitter*

Cooking Methods

Cooking Methods	Pàangyahmfaat	烹調法
bake	guhk	焗
boil	jyú, saahp	煮，燴
boil (water, soup)	bòu	煲
braise	hùhngsìu	紅燒
Cantonese hot pot	dá bìn lòuh	打邊爐
deep-fried	ja, jaau	炸
double boil	dahng	燉
grill	sìuhàau	燒烤
Mongolian hot pot	fówò	火鍋
pan-fried	jìn	煎
roast	sìu	燒
simmer	maahnfójyú	慢火煮
smoke	fàn	燻
steam	jìng	蒸
stew	màn	炆
stir-fried	cháau	炒

Dim-Sum

Dim-Sum	Dím sàm	點心
steamed rice flour rolls with barbecued pork	chàsìu chéung(fán)	叉燒腸（粉）
steamed barbecued pork bun	chàsiubàau	叉燒包

169

deep fried spring rolls with pork, chicken and bamboo shoot	chēungyún	春卷
stuffed cake with egg-yolk	chìnchàhnggòu	千層糕
custard tart	daahntāat	蛋撻
mashed lotus seed bun with egg-yolk	daahnwóng lìhnyùhng bāau	蛋黃蓮蓉包
mashed sesame seed bun with egg-yolk	daahnwóng màhyùhng bāau	蛋黃麻蓉包
steamed sweet egg pudding	dahng gàidáan	炖鷄蛋
double boiled fresh milk	dahng sèungpéi náaih	炖雙皮奶
steamed shrimps and bamboo shoot dumpling	fángwó	粉果
steamed chicken feet with soyed bean and chilli	fuhngjáau	鳳爪
steamed assorted meat and chicken rolls	gàijaat	鷄扎
steamed dumpling stuffed with pork and chicken soup	guntònggáau	灌湯餃
deep fried dumpling with pork, shrimp and bamboo shoot	hàahmséuigók	鹹水角
steamed shrimp dumpling	hàgáau	蝦餃

steamed fried rice in lotus leaf wrapping	hòhyihpfaahn	荷葉飯
lotus seed in red bean soup	lìhnjí hùhngdáusà	蓮子紅豆沙
almond bean curd and fruit	jaahpgwó dauhfuh	什菓豆腐
sweet mashed black sesame rolls	jìmàh gyún	芝蔴卷
glutinous rice dumpling wrapped in bamboo leaves	júng	粽
crisp and sticky sweet cake topped with walnut	máhjái	馬仔
steamed sponge cake	máhlàaigòu	馬拉糕
stuffed duck's web in oyster sauce	ngaapgeukjaat	鴨脚扎
steamed tripe in black beans and chilli sauce	ngàuhpaakyihp	牛柏葉
custard pudding	ngàuhyàuh guhk boudin	牛油焗布甸
steamed beef ball	ngàuhyuhk	牛肉
steamed dumpling filled with sweet coconut, peanuts & sesame	pàhnyihp gók	蘋葉角
steamed minced beef ball with bean curd skin	sàanjùk ngàuhyuhk	山竹牛肉

steamed pork chop with soyed bean sauce	sihjàp pàaihgwàt	豉汁排骨
steamed fresh cuttle fish	sìn yáu	鮮魷
deep fried bean curd roll with pork, shrimp in oyster sauce	sìnjùkgyún	鮮竹卷
steamed pork dumpling	sìu máai	燒賣
deep fried Taro dumplings	wuhgók	芋角
steamed sweet coconut pudding	yéhjàpgòu	椰汁糕
Sweet coconut glutinous cake	yèhsì nohmáihchìh	椰絲糯米糍
fried green pepper with pork or fish	yeuhng chèngjìu	釀青椒
steamed dumpling filled with shark's fin, pork and bamboo	yùhchigáau	魚翅餃

Drinks

	yámbán	飲品
black coffee	jàaifè	齋啡
bubbling wine	heijáu	汽酒
champagne	hèungbàn(jáu)	香檳（酒）
chocolate	jyùgùlìk	朱古力
cider	pìhnggwójáu	蘋菓酒
cocktail	gàiméihjáu	鷄尾酒
cocoa	gūkgú	哈咕
coffee	gafē	咖啡

172

condensed milk	lihnnáaih	煉奶
draught	sàangbe	生啤
fresh lemon juice	sinningjàp	鮮檸汁
fresh milk	sinnáaih	鮮奶
fruit juice	gwójàp	菓汁
fruit punch	jaahpgwó bànjih	什菓賓治
gin	jinjáu	毡酒
Guinness Stout	Bōdájáu	波打酒
Horlicks	Hóulahphāak	好立克
lemon tea	nihngmùngchàh	檸檬茶
lemonade	nihngmùngjāp	檸檬汁
milk	ngàuhnáaih	牛奶
milk powder	náaihfán	奶粉
mineral water	kwongchyùhnséui	礦泉水
orange juice	cháangjāp	橙汁
Ovaltine	Ngòwàhtihn	阿華田
red wine	hùhngjáu	紅酒
rum	làmjáu	冧酒
skimmed milk	tyutjìnáaih	脫脂奶
spirit, liquor	lihtjáu	烈酒
tea	chàh	茶
vodka	fuhkdahkgājáu	伏特加酒
Whisky	wàisihgéi	威士忌
white wine	baahkjáu	白酒
whole milk	chyùhnjìnáaih	全脂奶
wine	jáu	酒
Beer	Bējáu	啤酒
Blue Girl	Làahmmùi	藍妹
Blue Ribbon	Làahmdáai	藍帶
Budweiser	Baakwāi	百威
Carlsberg	Gāsihbaak	嘉士伯
Heineken	Héilihk	喜力
Kirin	Kèihlèuhn	麒麟
Lowenbaru	Lòuhwàhnbóu	盧雲堡
San Miguel	Sànglihk	生力
Tsing Tao	Chìngdóu	青島

Brandy	baahklàandéi	白蘭地
Bisquit V.S.O.P.	Baaksihgāt	百事吉
Courvoiser V.S.O.P.	Nàhpoleuhn	拿破崙
Hennesy X.O.	Hìnnèihsì	軒尼詩
Martell	Làahmdáai	藍帶
Remy Martin	Yàhntàuhmáh	人頭馬
Chinese wine	Jùnggwok jáu	中國酒
Bamboo-leaf Green	Jūkyihpchèng	竹葉青
Da Chu	Daaihkūk	大曲
Fen Jiu	Fàhnjáu	汾酒
Maotai	Màauhtòih	茅台
rice wine	máihjáu, sèungjìng	米酒，雙蒸
Wu Chia Pi	Nǵhgàpèih	五加皮
Soda	Héiséui	汽水
Coca Cola	(Hóháu)hólohk	（可口）可樂
Fanda	Fàndaaht	芬達
Green Spot	Luhkbóu	綠寶
Pepsi Cola	Baaksih hólohk	百事可樂
Schweppes	Yuhkchyùhn	玉泉
Seven up	Chàthéi	七喜
Sprite	Syutbīk	雪碧
Sunkist	Sànkèihsih	新奇士
Vita-soy	Wàihtànáaih	維他奶
Fruits	saanggwó	生果
apple	pìhnggwó	蘋果
apricot	hahng	杏
Australian pear	bēléi	啤梨
avocado	ngauhyàuhgwó	牛油果
banana	hèungjìu	香蕉
cantaloup	hèunggwà	香瓜

174

cherry	chèlèihjí	車厘子
coconut	yèhjí	椰子
dragon eye	lùhngngáan	龍眼
durian	làuhlihn	榴連
fig	mòuhfàgwó	無花果
grape	pòuhtàihjí	葡提子
grapefruit	sàiyáu	西柚
green apple	chèngpìhnggwó	青蘋果
guava	fàansehkláu	番石榴
honey dew melon	mahtgwà	蜜瓜
Kiwi Fruit	kèihyihgwó	奇異果
lemon	nìhngmùng	檸檬
lichee	laihjí	荔枝
loquat	pèihpàhgwó	枇杷果
Mandarin orange	gàm	柑
mango	mònggwó	芒果
mangosteen	sàanjùk	山竹
orange	cháang	橙
papaya	muhkgwà	木瓜
peach	tóu	桃
pear	léi	李
persimmon	nàhmchí	腍柿
pineapple	bòlòh	菠蘿
plum	boulàm, léi	布冧，李
pomelo	sàtìhnyáu, lūkyáu	沙田柚，碌柚
star-fruit	yèuhngtóu	洋桃
strawberry	sihdòbèiléi	士多啤梨
tangerine	gāt, gàmjái	桔，柑仔
water melon	sàigwà	西瓜

Kitchen Utensils	chyùhfóng yuhnggeuih	厨房用具
bowl	wún	碗
can-opener	guntáudòu	罐頭刀
chopper	choidòu	菜刀

175

chopping block	jàmbáan	砧板
chopsticks	faaijí	筷子
coffee pot	gafēwú	咖啡壺
earthenware cooking pot	sābòu	沙煲
egg cup	dáanbùi	蛋杯
egg-beater	dádáangèi	打蛋機
electric rice cooker	dihnfaahnbōu	電飯煲
fork	chà	叉
frying-pan	pìhngdáiwohk	平底鑊
glass	bùi	杯
kettle	chàhbòu	茶煲
knife	dòu	刀
microwave - oven	mèihbò guhklòuh	微波焗爐
mixer	gáaupuhnhei	搞拌器
napkin	chàangàn	餐巾
oil pitcher	yàuhjèun	油樽
oven	guhklòuh	焗爐
plate	díp, dihp	碟
refrigerator	syutgwaih	雪櫃
rice ladle	faahnhok	飯殼
sauce plate	meihdíp	味碟
soup ladle	tònghok	湯殼
soup pot (Chinese style)	wàhndíngbòu	雲頂煲
spatula	wohkcháan	鑊鏟
spoon	chìhgàng	瓷羹
steaming rack	jinglong, sunggá	蒸□，餸架
stove (L.P. gas)	sehkyàuhhei lòuh	石油汽爐
stove (electric)	dihnlòuh	電爐
stove (gas)	mùihhei lòuh	煤氣爐
strainer (for drying)	sāaugèi	筲箕
strainer (for frying)	jaaulèi	罩籬
strainer (tea)	chàhgaak	茶隔

176

table cloth	tóibou	枱布
teapot	chàhwú	茶壺
toaster	dòsilòuh	多士爐
tooth picks	ngàhchìm	牙簽
toothpick-holder	ngàhchìmtúng	牙簽筒
wok (Chinese cooking pan)	wohk	鑊

Noodle and Rice

Noodle and Rice	Faahnmihn	飯麵
Noodle (Cantonese style)	Mihn	麵
Braised noodle (per dish)	Baahnmihn	辦麵
with barbecued pork	chàsiu baahnmihn	叉燒辦麵
with brisket of beef	ngàuhláahm baahn-mihn	牛腩辦麵
with ginger & green	gèung chùng baahn mihn	薑葱辦麵
with mixed vegetables	lòhhon baahnmihn	羅漢辦麵
with mushroom	bākgù baahnmihn	北菇辦麵
with prawns	hàkàuh baahnmihn	蝦球辦麵
with shredded chicken	gàisì baahnmihn	鷄絲辦麵
E-Fu noodle (per dish)	Yìmihn	伊麵
stewed	gònsiu yìmihn	乾燒伊麵
with crab cream	háaihwòhng yìmihn	蟹黃伊麵
with crab meat	háaihyuhk yìmihn	蝦肉伊麵
Fried noodle (per dish)	Cháau mihn	炒麵
with barbecued pork	chàsiu cháau mihn	叉燒炒麵

177

with brisket of beef	ngàuhláahm cháau mihn	牛腩炒麵
with chicken balls	gàikàuh cháau mihn	鷄球炒麵
with garoupa balls	bàankàuh cháau mihn	斑球炒麵
with pork ribs	pàaihgwàt cháau mihn	排骨炒麵
with prawn balls	hàkàuh cháau mihn	蝦球炒麵
with shredded pork	yuhksì cháau mihn	肉絲炒麵
with sliced beef	ngàuhyuhk cháau mihn	牛肉炒麵
Noodles in soup (per bowl)	Tòngmihn	湯麵
with barbecued pork	chàsiu tòngmihn	叉燒湯麵
with braised duck's leg	ngaaptéui tòngmihn	鴨腿湯麵
With chicken balls	gàikàuh tòngmihn	鷄球湯麵
with ham	fótéui seuhngtòng sàangmihn	火腿上湯生麵
with pork ribs	pàaihgwàt tòngmihm	排骨湯麵
with roasted goose	sìungòh laaihfán	燒鵝瀬粉
with sliced beef	ngàuhyuhk tòngmihn	牛肉湯麵
with soyed chicken	yàuhgài tòngmihn	油鷄湯麵
Noddle in soup (per tureen)	Wòmihn	窩麵
with assorted meat	Yèuhngjàu wòmihn	楊州窩麵
with chicken balls	gàikàuh wòmihn	鷄球窩麵
with crab meat & egg	hùhngtòuh wòmihn	鴻圖窩麵

with garoupa balls	bāankàuh wòmihn	斑球窩麵
with shrimp balls	hàkàuh wòmihn	蝦球窩麵
Rice noodle (per dish)	Hó/máih fán	河/米粉
stewed rice-noodle with beef	gòncháau ngàuhhó	乾炒牛河
Vermicelli "Singapore" style	Sìngjàu cháaumaih	星洲炒米
Vermicelli "Fook Chow" style	Hahmùhn cháaumáih	廈門炒米
with beef	ngàuhyuhk cháauhó	牛肉炒河
with brisket of beef	ngàuhnáahm cháauhó	牛腩炒河
with sliced beef soyed bean and chilli	sihjìu ngàuhhó	豉椒牛河
Noodles in soup (northern style)	Tòngmihn	湯麵
diced chicken noodles	lyuhngài wùimihn	燉鷄煨麵
pekinese noodles with minced pork (without soup)	jajeung mihn	炸醬麵
pekinese noodles with mixed meat	daaihlóuhmihn	大滷麵
with mixed vegetables	soujaahpgám mihn	素什錦麵
with pork chop	pàaihgwàt mihn	排骨麵
with shredded chicken & ham	gàisì fótéui mihn	鷄絲火腿麵
with shredded pork and chinese pickles	jachoi yuhksì mihn	炸菜肉絲麵
with shredded pork and sour vegetables	syutchoi yuhksì mihn	雪菜肉絲麵

with shrimps	hàyàhn mihn	蝦仁麵
with sour & chilli sauce	syùnlaaht mihn	酸辣麵

Rice	Faahn	飯
Fried rice with assorted meat	Yèuhngjàu cháau faahn	楊州炒飯
with barbecued pork	chàsìufaahn	叉燒飯
with barbecued pork salty egg	hàahmdáan chàsìu faahn	咸蛋叉燒飯
with chicken ball & vegetable	choiyúhn gàikàuh faahn	菜遠鷄球飯
with curry brisket of beef	galēi ngaùhláahm faahn	咖喱牛肉飯
with curry chicken	galēigài faahn	咖喱鷄飯
with curry beef	galēi ngaùhyuhk faahn	咖喱牛肉飯
with diced meat & sweet corn	sūkmáih yuhknāp faahn	粟米肉粒飯
with diced pork and green peas	chèngdáu yuhknāp faahn	青豆肉粒飯
with fresh tomato and beef	sinké ngáu faahn	鮮茄牛飯
with garoupa ball and vegetable	choiyúhn bàankàuh faahn	菜遠斑球飯
with ham & fried egg	fótéui jìndáan faahn	火腿煎蛋飯
with minced beef & raw egg	wòdáan ngàuhyuhk faahn	窩蛋牛肉飯
with pork chop	jyùpá faahn	豬扒飯
with pork rib & vegetable	choiyúhn pàaihgwàt faahn	菜遠排骨飯
with prawn ball & vegetable	choiyúhn hàkàuh faahn	菜遠蝦球飯

with scrambled egg & shrimps	waahtdáan hàyàhn faahn	滑蛋蝦仁飯
with soyed chicken	yàuhgài faahn	油鷄飯
with steamed chicken	chitgài faahn	切鷄飯
with sweet corn and garoupa	sùkmáih bàanpín faahn	粟米斑片飯

Seafood	hóisin	海鮮
abalone	bàauyùh	鮑魚
carp	léihyú	鯉魚
clam	hín	蜆
crab	háaih	蟹
crabmeat	háaihyuhk	蟹肉
cuttle fish	mahkyùh	墨魚
eel	síhn	鱔
fish	yú	魚
garoupa	sehkbàanyú	石斑魚
jelly fish	hóijit	海蜇
lobster	lùhnghà	龍蝦
mussel	daahmchoi	淡菜
octopus	baatjáauyùh	八爪魚
oyster	hòuh	蠔
prawn	daaihhà	大蝦
red snapper	hùhngsàamyú	紅衫魚
salmon	sàammàhnyú	三文魚
scallop (dry)	gònyìuhchyúh	乾瑤柱
scallop (fresh)	daaijí	帶子
sea cucumber	hóisàm	海參
shark's fin	yùhchi	魚翅
shrimp	hà	蝦
sole	lùhngleih	龍脷
squid	yàuhyú	魷魚

| tuna fish | dyùnnàhyú | 端拿魚 |
| turtle | séuiyú | 水魚 |

Vegetables	sòchoi	蔬菜
apple cucumber, fuzzy melon	jitgwà, mòuhgwà	節瓜，毛瓜
arrowhead	chìhgù	茨菇
asparagus	louhséun	露筍
bamboo shoots	dùngséun	冬筍
bean sprouts	ngàhchoi	芽菜
bell pepper	dànglùhngjìu	燈籠椒
bitter melon	fúgwà	苦瓜
broccoli	sàilàahnfà	西蘭花
cabbage	yèhchoi	椰菜
carrot	gàmséun, hùhnglòhbaahk	甘筍，紅蘿蔔
cauliflower	yèhchoifà	椰菜花
celery	sàikàhn	西芹
Ceylon spinach	sàahnchoi	潺菜
chayote	fahtsáugwà	佛手瓜
Chinese box thorn	gáugéi	枸杞
Chinese broccoli	gaailáan	芥蘭
Chinese celery	kàhnchoi	芹菜
Chinese flowering cabbage	choisàm	菜心
Chinese parsley	yùhnsài	芫茜
Chinese spinach	yihnchoi	莧菜
chives	gáuchoi	韮菜
cucumber	chènggwà	青瓜
egg plant	ngáigwà	矮瓜
garlic	syuntàuh	蒜頭
ginger	gēung	薑
green pepper	chèngjiu	青椒
green radish	chènglòhbaahk	青蘿蔔

head lettuce	sài sàangchoi	西生菜
kudzu	fángot	粉葛
leek	syun	蒜
lettuce	sàangchoi	生菜
lotus root	lìhnngáuh	蓮藕
mushroom	chóugù, sìngú	草菇，鮮菇
mustard green	gaaichoi	芥菜
onion	yèuhngchùng	洋葱
pea shoots	dauhmiuh	豆苗
peas	hòhlàandáu	荷蘭豆
potato	syùhjái	薯仔
pumpkin	fàangwà, nàahmgwà	番瓜，南瓜
radish	hùhng(pèih)lòhbaahk	紅（皮）蘿蔔
red chilli	hùhnglaahtjìu	紅辣椒
scallions	gáuwòhng	韮黃
shallots	gònchùngtàuh	乾葱頭
silk melon, angled luffa	sìgwà	絲瓜
soybean sprouts	daaihdáu ngàhchoi	大豆芽菜
spinach	bòchoi	菠菜
spring onion	chùng	葱
stem ginger	jígèung	子薑
string bean	dauhgok	豆角
sweet corn	sūkmáih	粟米
sweet potato	fàansyú	番薯
taro	wuhtáu	芋頭
Tientsin cabbage	siuhchoi, wòhngngàhbaahk	紹菜，黃牙白
tomato	fàanké	蕃茄
turnip	lòhbaahk	蘿蔔
water chestnuts	máhtái	馬蹄
water cress	sàiyèuhngchoi	西洋菜
water spinach	ngungchoi, tùngchoi	甕菜，通菜
white cabbage	baahkchoi	白菜
white mushroom	baahkgù	白菇
wild rice shoots	gàauséun	膠筍
winter melon	dùnggwà	冬瓜

(5) Where to get help if you are sick

Medical Service and Health Terminology	Yìliuh Waihsàng Fuhkmouh seuhtyúh	醫療衛生服務術語
abnormal behaviour	yihsèuhng hàhngwàih	異常行為
accident and emergency section	gàpgau jùngsàm	急救中心
acupuncture treatment room	jàmgausāt	針灸室
ambulance	gausèungchè, sahpjihchè	救傷車，十字車
ambulance depot	gauwuhchè jaahm	救護車站
Auxiliary Medical Services	yìliuh fuhjohdéui	醫療輔助隊
bed	behngchòhng	病床
blood bank	hyutfu	血庫
blood gas analyser	yihmhyutyìh	驗血儀
casualty ward	gàpjingsàt	急症室
Chai Wan Health Centre	Chàaihwàan Gihnhòngyún	柴灣健康院
child assessment	yìhtùhng táinàhng jilìhk chàakyihm	兒童體能智力測驗
chiropractor	jekjèui jihlìuhsì	脊椎治療師
community physician	sèhkèuiyìhohk yìsàng	社區醫學醫生
community psychiatric nurse	jingsàhnfò sèhhòng wuhléih yàhnyùhn	精神科社康護理人員

184

community medicine	sèhkèuiyìhohk	社區醫學
Community Nursing Service Centre	Sèhhòng Wuhléih Jùngsàm	社康護理中心
consultant	jyúyahm gumahn yìsàng	主任顧問醫生
consulting room	chánjingsàt	診症室
convalescent home	lìuhyéuhngyún	療養院
custodial ward	gèilàuh behngfóng	羈留病房
dental clinic	ngàhfò chánsó	牙科診所
dental hygienist	ngàhchí waihsàngyùhn	牙齒衛生員
dental therapist	ngàhfò jihlìuhyùhn	牙科治療員
Director of Medical and Health Services	Yìmouhwaihsàngchyu Chyujéung	醫務衛生處處長
dispensary	yeuhkfòhng	藥房
enrolled nurse	dànggei wuhsih	登記護士
evening clinic service	yehchán fuhkmouh	夜診服務
externship	fèijyuyún sahtjaahp	非駐院實習
eye clinic	ngáahnfò chánlìuhsó	眼科診療所
Families Visiting Medical Office	Gùngmouhyùhngàsuhk chánlìuhsó	公務員家屬診療所
Family Health Service Centre	Móuhyìng Gihnhòngyún	母嬰健康院
fellowship examination	yúnsih háausìh	院士考試
first aid service	gausèung fuhkmouh	救傷服務
first class ward	tàuhdáng behngfóng	頭等病房
follow-up	fùkchán	覆診
free medical treatment	mìhnfai yìlìuh	免費醫療
general clinic (government)	póutùngfò mùhnchán	普通科門診
general hospital	póutùngfò yìyún	普通科醫院
general ward	póutùng behngfóng, daaihfóng	普通病房，大房

185

government hospital	jingfú yìyún	政府醫院
Government Community Nursing Service	Jingfú Séhhòng Wuhléih Fuhkmouh	政府社康護理服務
government laboratory	jingfú fayihmsó	政府化驗所
government chemist	jingfú fayihmsì	政府化驗師
government health warning	jingfú gihnhòng jùnggou	政府健康忠告
half-way house	jùngtòuh sūkséh	中途宿舍
health and medical services	yìliuh waihsàng fuhkmouh	醫療衛生服務
health centre	gihnhòngyún	健康院
health education	gihnhòng gaauyuhk	健康教育
herbalist	jùngyì	中醫
Hong Kong Psychiatric Centre	Hèunggóng Jìngsàhnbehng Chánliuhsó	香港精神病診療所
Hong Kong Anti-cancer Society	Hèunggóng Fòhngngàahmwúi	香港防癌會
Hong Kong College of General Practitioners	Hèunggóng Chyùhnfò Yìhohkyún	香港全科醫學院
Hong Kong Dental Association	Hèunggóng Ngàhyìhohkwúi	香港牙醫學會
Hong Kong Medical Association	Hèunggóng Yìhohkwúi	香港醫學會
Hong Kong Red Cross Blood Transfusion Service	Hèunggóng Hùhngsahpjihwúi syùhyut fuhkmouhjùngsàm	香港紅十字會輸血服務中心
Hong Kong Red Cross Society	Hèunggóng Hùhngsahpjihwúi	香港紅十字會
hospital administrator	yúnmouh jyúyahm	院務主任

hospital admission certificate	yahpyún jingmìhngsyù	入院證明書
hospital discharge certificate	chèutyún jingmìhngsyù	出院證明書
hospitalization	lauhyúnchánjih	留院診治
infirmary	wuhyéuhngyún	護養院
innoculation centre	jyusehjaahm	注射站
intensive care unit	sàmchitjihlìuh behngfóng	深切治療病房
isolation ward	gaaklèih behngfóng	隔離病房
Kwai Chung Hospital	Kwàihchùng Yìyún	葵涌醫院
leprosy clinic	màhfùng chánlìuhsó	麻瘋診療所
Maclehose Medical Rehablitation Centre	Mahklèihhouh Fuhkhòngyún	麥理浩復康院
Margaret Trench Medical Rehabilitation Centre	Daailèuhnjìfùyàhn Fuhkhòngyún	載麟趾夫人復康院
maternal unit	cháanfòbouh	產科部
maternity home	làuhcháansó	留產所
medicaid	yìyeuhk wùhnjoh	醫藥援助
Medical and Health Department	Yìmouhwaihsàngchyu	醫務衛生處
medical care	yìlìuh fuhkmouh	醫療服務
medical certificate	yìsàng jingmìhngsyù	醫生證明書
medical congress	yìhohk wuihyíh	醫學會議
Medical Council	Yìmouh wáiyùhnwúi	醫務委員會
Medical Development Advisory Committee	Yìmouhfaatjìn Jìsèun Wáiyùhnwúi	醫務發展咨詢委員會
medical ethics	yìdàk	醫德

medical examina- tion	táigaak gimyihm	體格檢驗
medical labora- tory technician	yìliuhsahtyihmsàt geihseuhtyùhn	醫療實驗室 技術員
medical personnel	yìmouh yàhnyùhn	醫務人員
medical service	yìliuh fuhkmouh	醫療服務
medical social work	yìmouh séhwúigùngjok	醫務社會工 作
Methadone Detoxification Clinic	Méihsàtùhng Gaaiduhk Chánsó	美沙酮戒毒 診所
motorcycle ambulance support system	gauwuh dihndàanchè jiwùhn gaiwaahk	救護電單車 支援計劃
nurse training school	wuhsih fanlihn hohkhaauh	護士訓練學 校
Nursing Officer	wuhléih jyúyahm	護理主任
nursing staff	wuhléihyàhnyùhn	護理人員
operation theatre	sáuseuhtsàt	手術室
optometrical profession	sihgwònghohk	視光學
oral health clinic	háuhòng gihnhòng chánsó	口腔健康診 所
Orthopaedic and Traumatic Surgery Depart- ment	Giuyìhngngoihfò kahp Chongsèunghohk haih	矯形外科及 創傷學系
out-patient clinic / depart- ment	mùhnchánbouh	門診部
overseas medical qualifications	hóingoih yìhohk jìgaak	海外醫學資 格
para-medical staff	fuhjoh yìliuh yàhnyùhn	輔助醫療人 員
personal hygiene	goyàhn waihsàng	個人衛生

physical medicine unit	yìliuh fuhkhòngyún	醫療復康院
polyclinic	fànfò chánsó	分科診所
Port Health Office	Góngháu Waihsàngchyu	港口衛生處
private hospital	sìgà yìyún	私家醫院
psychiatric centre	Jìngsàhnbehng Jihlìuhjùngsàm	精神病治療中心
public hospital	gùnglahp yìyún	公立醫院
quarantine station	gìmyìhkjaahm	檢疫站
Radiation Board	Fongsehmahtjàt Gúnléihgúk	放射物質管理局
radiodiagnostic department	fongseh chándyunbouh	放射診斷部
regional hospital	fànkèui yìyún	分區醫院
registered nurse	jyuchaak wuhsih	註冊護士
rehabaid centre	fuhkhòngyuhnggeuih jùngsàm	復康用具中心
scanner unit	dihnnóuh soumìuhbouh	電腦掃描部
school children's dental clinic	hohktùhng ngàhfò chánsó	學童牙科診所
School Dental Care Service	hohktùhng ngàhchíbóugihn gaiwaahk	學童牙齒保健計劃
social hygiene clinic	séhwúi waihsàngfò chánsó	社會衛生科診所
specialist clinic	jyùnfò mùhnchán	專科門診
St. John Ambulance Association and Brigade	Singyeukhohn Gausèungwúi kei Gausèungdéui	聖約翰救傷會暨救傷隊
student nurse	wuhsih hohksàang	護士學生
subvented hospital	bóujoh yìyún	補助醫院
surveillance system	gàamchaat jóujìk	監察組織
teaching hospital	gaauhohk yìyún	教學醫院

tuberculosis and chest clinic	hùngfai chánliuhsó	胸肺診療所
ward	behngfóng	病房
wheel-chair	lèuhnyí	輪椅

Hospitals   Yìyún   醫院

Baptist Hospital	Jamwúi Yìyún	浸會醫院
Canossa Hospital	Gànoksaat Yìyún	嘉諾撒醫院
Caritas Medical Center	Mìhngngoi Yìyún	明愛醫院
Castle Peak Hospital	Chìngsàan Yìyún	青山醫院
Christain United Hospital	Lyùhnhahp Yìyún	聯合醫院
Duchess of Kent Childrens' Hospital	Gàndàk Gùngjeukfù- yàhn Yìhtùhng Yìyún	根德公爵夫人 兒童醫院
Elizabeth Hospital	Yìleihsàbaak Yìyún	伊利沙白醫院
Evangel Hospital	Bodouh Yìyún	播道醫院
Grantham Hospital	Gotleuhnghùhng Yìyún	葛量洪醫院
Haven of Hope Hospital	Lìhngsaht Yìyún	靈實醫院
HK Adventist Hospital	Góngngòn Yìyún	港安醫院
HK Buddhist Hospital	Hèunggóng Fahtgaau Yìyún	香港佛教醫院
HK Central Hospital	Góngjùng Yìyún	港中醫院
Hong Kong Sanatorium and Hospital	Yéuhngwòh Yìyún	養和醫院
Kowloon Hospital	Gàulùhng Yìyún	九龍醫院

190

Kwong Wah Hospital	Gwóngwàh Yìyún	廣華醫院
Matilda and War Memorial Hospital	Mìhngdàk Yìyún	明德醫院
Nam Long Hospital	Nàahmlóhng Yìyún	南朗醫院
Nethersole Hospital	Nàhdàsou Yìyún	那打素醫院
Our Lady of Maryknoll Hospital	Singmóuh Yìyún	聖母醫院
Pok Oi Hospital	Bokngoi Yìyún	博愛醫院
Precuious Blood Hospital	Bóuhyut Yìyún	寶血醫院
Prince of Wales Hospital	Wàiyìhsì Chànwòhng Yìyún	威爾斯親王醫院
Prince Philip Dental Hospital	Fèilihpchànwòhng Ngàhfò Yìyún	菲臘親王牙科醫院
Princess Margaret Hospital	Máhgàliht Yìyún	瑪嘉烈醫院
Queen Mary Hospital	Máhlaih Yìyún	瑪麗醫院
Ruttonjee Sanatorium	Leuhtdēunjih Lìuhyéuhngyún	律敦治療養院
St. Paul's Hospital	Singbóuluhk Yìyún (Faatgwok Yìyun)	聖保羅醫院 (法國醫院)
St. Teresa's Hospital	Singdāklaahksaat Yìyún	聖德肋撒醫院
Tang Shiu Kin Hospital	Dahngsiuhgìn Yìyún	鄧肇堅醫院
Tsuen Wan Adventist Hospital	Chyùhnwàan Góng-ngòn Yìyún	荃灣港安醫院
Tung Wah Eastern Hospital	Dùngwàh Dùngyún	東華東院
Tung Wah Hospital	Dùngwàh Yìyún	東華醫院
Yan Chai Hospital	Yàhnjai Yìyún	仁濟醫院

Parts of the Body
Sàntáigokbouh fahn 身體各部份

abdomen	tóuh, fūk	肚，腹
ankle	geukngáahn	脚眼
appendix	làahnméih	闌尾
arm	(sáu) bei	（手）臂
artery	duhngmahk	動脈
anus	gòngmùhn	肛門
brain	nóuh	腦
back	bui	背
bronchi	jìheigún	支氣管
bladder	pòhnggwòng	膀胱
bone	gwàt	骨
blood	hyut	血
blood vessel	hyutgún	血管
breast	hùng, sàmháu	胸，心口
cheek	mihn	面
chin	hahpàh	下巴
chest	hùng	胸
calf	síutéui	小腿
caecum	màahngchéung	盲腸
cervix uteri	jígùnggéng	子宮頸
diaphram	wàahnggaakmók	橫隔膜
duoderum	sahpyih jíchèuhng	十二指腸
ear	yíh, yìhjái	耳，耳仔
ear lobe	yíhjyù, yíhsèuih	耳珠，耳垂
eyes	ngáahn	眼
eyebrow	ngáahnmèih	眼眉
eyelashes	ngáahnjihtmòuh	眼捷毛
elbow	sáujàang, jáau	手踭，肘
foot	geuk	脚
forearm	chìhnbei	前臂
finger	sáují	手指
fingernails	sáujígaap	手指甲

fallopian tube	syùléungún	輸卵管
gum	ngàhyuhk	牙肉
gland	sin	腺
gall bladder	dáam (nòhng)	胆（囊）
head	tàuh	頭
hair (fine)	mòuh	毛
hair (on the head)	tàuhfaat	頭髮
hard palate	seuhngngohk	上顎
heart	sàm	心
heart valves	sàmfáan	心瓣
heel	geukjàang	脚踭
hand	sáu	手
instep	geukbui	脚背
intestine, large	daaihchéung	大腸
intestine, small	síuchéung	小腸
jaw	hahp, hahpàh	頜，下巴
joint	gwàanjit	關節
kidney	sáhn, yiu	腎，腰
knee	sàt (tàuh)	膝（頭）
lip	(háu)sèuhn	（口）唇
larynx	yìn, hàuhlùhng	咽，喉嚨
lung	fai	肺
liver	gòn	肝
leg	téui, geuk	腿，脚
mouth	háu, jéui	口，嘴
muscle	gèiyuhk	肌肉
mucous membrane	nìmmók	黏膜
nose	beih(gō)	鼻（哥）
neck	géng	頸
nerve	sàhngìng	神經
nipple	náaihtàuh	奶頭
oesophagus	sihkdouh	食道
ovary	léunchàauh	卵巢
pleura	hùngmók, lahkmóh	胸膜，肋膜
pancreas	yìh(sin)	胰（腺）
palm	sáujéung	手掌

prostate gland	chìhnlihtsin,	前列腺，
	sipwuhsin	攝護腺
penis	yàmging	陰莖
prepuce	bàaupèih	包皮
rectum	jihkchéung	直腸
rib	lahkgwàt	肋骨
senses	jigok	知覺
hearing	ting gok	聽覺
smell (n)	meih gok	味覺
taste (v)	simeihdouh	試味道
touch	jūk gok	觸覺
vision	sih gok	視覺
skull	tàuh(lòuh)gwàt	頭（顱）骨
shoulder	boktàuh, gin	膊頭，肩
spleen	pèih	脾
stomach	waih	胃
scrotum	yàmnòhng	陰囊
spine (vertebra)	jekchyúh, jekjèui	脊柱，脊椎
scalp	tàuhpèih	頭皮
skin	pèih	皮
spinal cord	jekseuih	脊髓
throat	hàuhlùhng	喉嚨
thyroid gland	gaapjohngsin	甲狀腺
tonsils	hàuhwát, bíntòuhsin	喉核，扁桃腺
trachea	heigún	氣管
thumb	sáujígùng, móuhjí	手指公，母指
thigh	daaihbéi, daaihtéui	大脾，大腿
toes	geukjí	脚趾
toenails	geuk(jí)gaap	脚（趾）甲
testis	gòuyún	睪丸
tongue	leih, siht	脷，舌
upper arm	seuhngbei	上臂
ureter	syùniuhgún	輸尿管
urethra	niuhdouh	尿道
uterus	jígùng	子宮
vein	jihngmahk	靜脈
vagina	yàmdouh	陰道

194

vasdeferens	syùjìnggún	輸精管
wrist	sáuwún	手腕
waist	yìu	腰
circulatory system	chèuhnwàahn haihtúng	循環系統
digestive system	sìufa haihtúng	消化系統
endocrine system	noihfànbei haihtúng	內分泌系統
muscular system	gèiyuhk haihtúng	肌肉系統
nervous system	sàhngìng haihtúng	神經系統
reproductive system	sàngjihk haihtúng	生殖系統
respiratory system	fùkàp haihtúng	呼吸系統
skeletal system	gwàtgaak haihtúng	骨骼系統
urinary system	pàaihniuh haihtúng	排尿系統

(6) How to plan for a trip

aviation [handwritten]

Air Lines Companies	Hòhnghùnggūngsi	航空公司
Air France	Faatgwok Hòhng-hùng gūngsi	法國航空公司
Air India	Yandouh Hòhnghùnggūngsi	印度航空公司
Air Lanka	Sìléihlàahnkà Hòhnghùnggūngsi	斯里蘭卡航空公司
Air Nauru	Nàhnóuh Hòhnghùnggūnsi	那魯航空公司
Air New Zealand	Náusàilàahn Hòhnghùnggūngsi	紐西蘭航空公司
Air Niugini *New Guinea* [handwritten]	Sàngèinoihnga Hòhnghùnggūngsi	新畿內亞航空公司
Alitalia Airlines	Yidaaihleih Hòhnghúnggūngsi	意大利航空公司
All Nippon Airways	Chyùhn yaht hùng Hòhnghùng gūngsi	全日空航空公司
British Airways	Yinggwok Hòhnghùnggūngsi	英國航空公司
British Caledonian Airways	Yinggwok Gàmsi Hòhnghùnggūngsi *gold lion* [handwritten]	英國金獅航空公司
Canadian Pacific Air	Gànàhdaaih Taaipìhngyèuhng Hòhnghùnggūngsi	加拿大太平洋航空公司
Cathay Pacific Airways	Gwoktaai *(huge)* [handwritten] Hòhnghùnggūngsi	國泰航空公司
China Airlines	Jùngwàh Hòhnghùnggūngsi	中華航空公司

old word for China [handwritten, left margin]

country [handwritten]

super [handwritten] *first* [handwritten] *ocean* [handwritten]

(belongs to Taiwan + ∴ no gwok) [handwritten]

196

China National Aviation Corp.	Jùnggwok màhnhòhng	中國民航
Continental Airlines	Méihgwok Daaihluhk Hòhnghùnggūngsì	美國大陸航空公司
Delta Airlines	Sàamgokjàu Hòhnghùnggūngsì	三角洲航空公司
Dragon Air	Gónglùhng Hòhnghùnggūngsì	港龍航空公司
Garuda Indonesian Airways	Gànóuhdaaht Yannèih Hòhnghùnggūngsì	嘉魯達印尼航空公司
Gulf Air	Hóiwàan Hòhnghùnggūngsì	海灣航空公司
Japan Air Lines	Yahtbún Hòhnghùnggūngsì	日本航空公司
KLM Royal Dutch Airlines	Hòhlāan Hòhnghùnggūngsì	荷蘭航空公司
Korean Air	Daaihhòhn Hòhnghùnggūngsì	大韓航空公司
Lufthansa German Airlines	Dākgwok Hòhnghùnggūngsì	德國航空公司
Malaysian Airline System	Máhlòihsàinga Hòhnghùnghaihtúng	馬來西亞航空公司
Northwest Orient Airlines	Sàibàk Hòhnghùnggūngsì	西北航空公司
Philippine Airlines	Fèileuhtbàn Hòhnghùnggūngsì	菲律賓航空公司
Quantas Airways	Ngoujàu Hòhnghùnggūngsì	澳洲航空公司
Royal Brunei Airlines	Wòhnggà Màhnlòih Hòhnghùnggūngsì	皇家汶來航空公司
Singapore Airlines	Sàngabō Hòhnghùnggūngsì	新加坡航空公司
SouthAfrica Airways	Nàahmfèi Hòhnghùnggūngsì	南非航空公司
Swissair	Seuihsih Hòhnghùnggūngsì	瑞士航空公司

Thai International Airways	Taaigwok Gwokjai Hòhnghùnggūngsi	泰國國際航空公司
United Airlines	Lyùhnhahp Hòhnghùnggūngsi	聯合航空公司
Western Airlines	Sàifòng *West direction* Hòhnghùnggūngsi	西方航空公司

Banks

	Ngàhnhòhng	銀行
Bank of America	Méihgwok ngàhnhòhng	美國銀行
Bank of China	Jùnggwok ngàhnhòhng	中國銀行
Bank of Communication	Gàautùng ngàhnhòhng	交通銀行
Bank of Tokyo	Dùnggìng ngàhnhòhng	東京銀行
Banque Nationale De Paris	Faatgwok Gwokgà Bālàih ngàhnhòhng	法國國家巴黎銀行
Barclays Bank	Paakhāaklòih ngàhnhòhng	柏克萊銀行
Belgian Bank	Wàhbéi ngàhnhòhng	華比銀行
Fuji Bank	Fusih ngàhnhòhng	富士銀行
Hang Seng Bank	Hàhng sàng ngàhnhòhng	恒生銀行
Hong Kong & Shanghai Banking Corporation	Wuihfùng ngàhnhòhng	滙豐銀行
Standard Chartered Bank	Jàdá ngàhnhòhng	渣打銀行

wine

Hotels and Guest Houses

	Jáudim, Bàngún	酒店，賓館
Ambassador	Gwokbàn Jáudim	國賓酒店

Conrad Hotel =

Astor	Làahngùng Jáudim	蘭宮酒店
Bangkok Royal	Maahngūk Gwaibàn Jáudim	曼谷貴賓酒店
Caritas Bianchi Lodge	Mìhngngoi Baahkyìngkèih Bàngún	明愛白英奇賓館
Carlton	Wàhyìhdàng Jáudim	華爾登酒店
Cathay	Gwoktaai Jáudim	國泰酒店
Cheung Chau Warwick	Wàhwài Jáudim	華威酒店
Chung Hing	Jùnghìng Jáudim	中興酒店
Chungking House	Chùhnghìng Jìudoihsó	重慶招待所
Empress	Daihauh Jáudim	帝后酒店
Excelsior	Yìhdùng Jáudim	怡東酒店
First	Daihyāt Jáudim	第一酒店
Fortuna	Fudōu Jáudim	富都酒店
Fortuna Court	Fudōugok Jáudim	富都閣酒店
Fuji	Fusih Jáudim	富士酒店
Furama	Fulaihwàh Jáudim	富麗華酒店
Galaxie	Gàlòih Jáudim	嘉來酒店
Golden Gate	Gàmmuhn Jáudim	金門酒店
Grand	Gaaklàahn Jáudim	格蘭酒店
Harbour	Wàhgwok Jáudim	華國酒店
Harbour View International House	Wàangíng Gwokjai Bàngún	灣景國際賓館
Hilton	Hèiyìhdéun/deuhn Jáudim	希爾頓酒店
Holiday Inn Golden Mile	Gàmwihk Gayaht Jáudim	金域假日酒店
Holiday Inn Harbour View	Hóigíng Gayaht Jáudim	海景假日酒店
HongKong	Hèunggóng Jáudim	香港酒店
Hyatt Regency	Hóiyuht Jáudim	凱悅酒店
Imperial	Daigwok Jáudim	帝國酒店
International	Gwokjai Jáudim	國際酒店

199

King's	Gòungáh Jáudim	高雅酒店
Kowloon	Gáulùhng Jáudim	九龍酒店
Lee Gardens	Leihyún Jáudim	利園酒店
Luk Kwok	Luhkgwok Faahndim	六國飯店
Mandarin	Màhnwàh Jáudim	文華酒店
Marco Polo	Máhgòbuhtlòh Jáudim	馬哥勃羅酒店
Merlin	Méihlèuhn Jáudim	美輪酒店
Miramar	Méihlaihwàh Jáudim	美麗華酒店
Nathan	Nèihdèun Jáudim	彌敦酒店
New World	Sànsaigaai Jáudim	新世界酒店
Palace	Gàmgok Jáudim	金閣酒店
Park	Baaklohk Jáudim	百樂酒店
Park Lane	Paaknìhng Jáudim	栢寧酒店
Pearl Island	Lùhngjyùdóu Jáudim	龍珠島酒店
Peninsula	Bundóu Jáudim	半島酒店
Prince	Taaijí Jáudim	太子酒店
Regal Meridien	Fuhòuh Jáudim	富豪酒店
Regal Meridien Airport	Fuhòuh Gèichèuhng Jáudim	富豪機場酒店
Regent	Laihjìng Jáudim	麗晶酒店
Ritz	Lohksì Jáudim	樂斯酒店
Riverside Plaza	Laihhòuh Jáudim	麗豪酒店
Royal Garden	Daiyún Jáudim	帝苑酒店
Shamrock	Sànlohk Jáudim	新樂酒店
Shangri-La	Hèunggaakléihlāai Jáudim	香格里拉酒店
Singapore	Sàngabō Jáudim	新加坡酒店
Y.M.C.A.	Chìngnìhnwúi, Sàichìngwúi	靑年會，西靑會
Y.W.C.A.	Néuihchìngnìhnwúi	女靑年會

Major Cities in China	Jùnggwok jyúyiu sìhngsíh	中國主要城市
Beijing	Bākgìng	北京

Chengdu	Sìhngdōu	成都
Chongqing	Chùhnghing	重慶
Guangzhou	Gwóngjàu	廣州
Guilin	Gwailàhm	桂林
Hangzhou	Hòhngjàu	杭州
Harbin	Hāyíhbàn	哈爾濱
Huhhot	Fùwòhhouhdahk	呼和浩特
Jinan	Jainàahm	濟南
Kunming	Kwànmìhng	昆明
Nanjing	Nàahmgìng	南京
Shanghai	Seuhnghói	上海
Shenyang	Sámyèuhng	瀋陽
Shenzhen	Sàmjan	深圳
Taibei, Taipei	Tòihbāk	台北
Tienjing	Tìnjèun	天津
Urumqi	Wùlóuhmuhkchàih	烏魯木齊
Wuhan	Móuhhon	武漢
Xiamen	Hahmùhn	廈門
Xian	Sàingòn	西安

Major Cities in the World

Saigaai jyúyiu sìhngsih

世界主要城市

Aden	Ngadìng	亞丁
Amsterdam	Amóuhsidahkdāan	亞姆斯特丹
Athens	Ngáhdín	雅典
Bangkok	Maahngūk	曼谷
Beijing	Bākgìng	北京
Belfast	Buiyíhfaatsìdahk	貝爾法斯特
Belgrade	Buiyíhgaaklòihdāk	貝爾格萊得
Berlin	Paaklàhm	柏林
Bermuda	Baakmouhdaaht	百慕達
Bogota	Bògòdaaih	波哥大
Bohn	Bòyàn	波恩
Bombay	Maahngmáaih	孟買

201

Boston	Bōsihdéun	波士頓
Brasilia	Bàsaileihnga	巴西利亞
Brussels	Boulóuhchoiyih	布魯塞爾
Budapest	Boudaahtpuisi	布達佩斯
Buenos Aires	Bouyihnoksìngaaih-	布宜諾斯艾利
	leihsì	斯
Cairo	Hòilòh	開羅
Calcutta	Gāyíhgokdaap	加爾各答
Capetown	Hòipóudèun	開普敦
Caracas	Gālaaigāsì	加拉加斯
Chicago	Jigāgò	芝加哥
Colombo	Gòlèuhnbò	哥倫波
Copenhagen	Gòbúnhāgàn	哥本哈根
Dakar	Daahtkaakyíh	達喀爾
Damascus	Daaihmáhsihgaak	大馬士革
Darwin	Daahtyíhmàhn	達爾文
Delhi	Dākléih	德里
Detroit	Dáidahkleuht	底特律
Dublin	Dōupaaklàhm	都柏林
Frankfurt	Faatlàahnhāakfùk	法蘭克福
Geneva	Yahtnoihngáh	日內瓦
Glasgow	Gaaklàaisìgò	格拉斯哥
Guadalajara	Gwàdaahtlàaihālàai	瓜達拉哈拉
Guam	Gwàandóu	關島
Guatemala	Ngàihdeihmáhlàai	危地馬拉
Havana	Hahwāannàh	夏灣拿
Helsinki	Hāakyíhsàngèi	赫爾辛基
Hong Kong	Hèunggóng	香港
Honolulu	Tàahnhèungsàan	壇香山
Houston	Hàuhsìdéun	侯斯頓
Islamabad	Yísilàahnbóu	伊斯蘭堡
Jakarta	Yèhgàdaaht	耶加達
Jerusalem	Yèhlouhsaatláahng	耶路撒冷
Johannesburg	Yeukhohnnèihsìbóu	約翰尼斯堡
Kabul	Kaakbouyíh	喀布爾
Kaula Lumpur	Gātlùhngbò	吉隆坡
Kiev	Gèifuh	基輔

Kobe	Sàhnwuh	神戶
Kuwait	Fōwàidahk	科威特
La Paz	Làaibāsi	拉巴斯
Las Vegas	Làaisìwàihgāsi/	拉斯維加斯
	dóusìhng	/賭城
Leningrad	Lihtnìhnggaaklaahk	列寧格勒
Lima	Leihmáh	利馬
Lisbon	Léihsìbún	里斯本
Liverpool	Leihmahtpóu	利物浦
London	Lèuhndèun	倫敦
Los Angeles	Lokchaamgèi/Lòhsáang	洛杉磯/羅省
Lyons	Léihngòhng	里昂
Madrid	Máhdākléih	馬德里
Manila	Máhnèihlāai	馬尼拉
Marseille	Máhchoi	馬賽
Melbourne	Mahkyíhbut	墨爾砵
Mexico City	Mahksàigōsìhng	墨西哥城
Miami	Maaihngaméih	邁亞美
Milan	Máihlàahn	米蘭
Montreal	Múhndeihhó	滿地可
Moscow	Mohksifò	莫斯科
Munich	Mouhnèihhāak	慕尼克
New York	NáuYeuk	紐約
Osaka	Daaihbáan	大坂
Oslo	Ngousìluhk	奧斯陸
Panama	Bànàhmáhsìhng	巴拿馬城
Paris	Bàlàih	巴黎
Penang	Bànsìhng	檳城
Perth	Puisì	佩思
Philadelphia	Faisìhng	費城
Pnom Penh	Gàmbìn	金邊
Prague	Boulāaigaak	布拉格
Quito	Gēidò	基多
Rangoon	Yéuhnggwòng	仰光
Rio de Janeiro	Léihyeukyihtnoihlòuh	里約熱內盧
Rome	Lòhmáh	羅馬
Saigon	Sàigung	西貢

San Francisco	Sàamfàahnsíh/	三藩市/舊金
	Gauhgàmsàan	山
Santiago	Singdeihngàhgò	聖地牙哥
Seattle	Sàingáhtòuh	西雅圖
Seoul	Honsìhng	漢城
Shanghai	Seuhnghói	上海
Singapore	Sàngabò	新加坡
Stockholm	Sìdākgòyíhmò	斯德哥爾摩
Sydney	Syutlèih	雪梨
Tehran, Teheran	Dākhàaklàahn	德黑蘭
Tel Aviv	tòihlāaiwàihfù	台拉維夫
Tokyo	Dùnggìng	東京
Toronto	Dòlèuhndò	多倫多
Vancouver	Wàngòwàh	溫哥華
Venice	Wāinèihsī	威尼斯
Vienna	Wàihyáhnaahp	維也納
Warsaw	Wàhsà	華沙
Washington D.C.	Wàhsìhngdeuhn/Wàhfú	華盛頓/華府
Wellington	Wàinìhngdeuhn	威靈頓
Zurich	Sòulàihsai	蘇黎世

(7) How to find out what's happening

Mass Media	Daaihjung Mùihgaai	大眾媒介
advertising control	gwónggou gúnjai	廣告管制
advertising agent	gwónggou gùngsì	廣告公司
air (v)	bofong	播放
air photograph	hùngjùngsipyíng jiupín	空中攝影照片
airport conference room	gèichèuhng geijésāt	機場記者室
anti-piracy committee	fáandouhyan síujóu	反盜印小組
approved for exhibition	pàijéun gùngyíng	批准公映
ban	gamyíng	禁映
broadcast by satellite	yàhnjouhwaihsìng jyúnbo	人造衛星轉播
broadcast live	yihnchèuhng jihkbo	現場直播
broadcast picture	dihnsih wámín	電視畫面
Broadcasting Review Board	Gwóngbosihyihp Gímtóu Wáiyùhnwúi	廣播事業檢討委員會
cable systems	yàuhsin chyùhnbohaihtúng	有線傳播系統
cable television	yàuhsin dihnsih	有線電視
censorship	sànmàhn gímchàh	新聞檢查
children's programme	yìhtùhng jitmuhk	兒童節目
Chinese language typesetting	Jùngmàhn pàaihjih	中文排字
circulation	siulouh	銷路
commercial advertising	sèungyihp gwónggou	商業廣告

commercials	gwónggoupín	廣告片
compact / digital audio disc system	lùihseh soumáh cheungpín haihtúng	鐳射數碼唱片系統
compere	jitmuhk jyúchìhyàhn	節目主持人
copyright infringement	chàmfaahn báankyùhn	侵犯版權
copyright	báankyuhn	版權
copywriter	jaangóuyàhn	撰稿人
current affairs programme	sihsih jitmuhk	時事節目
data transmission	sougeui chyùhnsung	數據傳送
deadline	jihtgóu sìhgaan	截稿時間
direct satellite transmissions	yàhnjouhwaihsìng jihkjip jyúnbo	人造衛星直接轉播
Director of Information Services	Sànmàhnchyu Chyujéung	新聞處處長
Director of Boardcasting	Gwóngbochyúh Chyúhjéung	廣播處處長
disc jockey	cheungpín kèhsi	唱片騎師
drama series	kehkjaahp	劇集
editing	pìnchàp gùngjok	編輯工作
electronic media	dihnji mùihgaai	電子媒介
enfranchised commercial broadcast tele-vision station	dahkhéui sèungyihp dihnsihtòih	特許商業電視台
enrichment programme	yìkji jitmuhk	益智節目
exposure	bouhgwòng chìhngdouh	曝光程度
facsimile machine	chyùhnjàngèi	傳真機
family viewing hours (TV)	hahpgàfùn sìhgaan	合家歡時間
feature article	dahkgóu	特稿
Film Censorship Regulations	Dihnyíng Gímchàh Kwàilaih	電影檢查規例

film editing	dihnyíng jínchàp	電影剪輯
FM broadcasting	tiuhpàhn gwóngbo	調頻廣播
foreign news agency	ngoihgwok sànmàhnséh	外國新聞社
free air time	mihnfai boyíng sihgaan	免費播影時間
freelance writer	jihyàuh jokgà	自由作家
front page head-line	tàuhtiuhsànmán	頭條新聞
government programme	jingfú sipjai jitmuhk	政府攝製節目
home viewer	gàtihng gùnjung	家庭觀衆
Hong Kong Journa-lists' Associa-tion	Hèunggóng Geijé Hipwúi	香港記者協會
interference	gònyíu	干擾
location filming	paaksip ngoihgíng	拍攝外景
mass communica-tion	daaihjung chyùhnbo	大衆傳播
mass media	daaihjung mùihgaai	大衆媒介
media photogra-pher	sipyíng geijé	攝影記者
mobile radio	làuhduhng deuigónggèi	流動對講機
morning post	jóubou	早報
multiplex sound system	dòsìngdouh buhnyàmhaihtúng	多聲道伴音系統
multiplex sound-casting	dòsìngdouh gwóngbo	多聲道廣播
news headlines	sànmàhn tàihyiu	新聞提要
news report	sànmàhn bougou	新聞報告
no comment	mòuh hó fuhnggou	無可奉告
not recommended for young children	yìhtùhng bātyìh	兒童不宜
overhead projec-tor	gòuyínggèi	高映機

Panal of Film Censors	Dihnyíng Gímchàhchyu	電影檢查處
photostated / xeroxed copy	yíngyanbún	影印本
pirate	douhyanyàhn	盜印人
poor reception	jipsàu haauhgwó chà	接收效果差
poster	hóibou	海報
press and publicity manager	sànmàhn kahp syùnchyùhn jyúyahm	新聞及宣傳主任
press briefing	sànmàhn gáanbouwúi	新聞簡報會
press conference	geijé jìudoihwúi	記者招待會
prime time	wòhnggàm sìhgaan	黃金時間
programme promos	jitmuhk syùnchyùhnpín	節目宣傳片
public affairs programme	gùngguhng sihmouh jitmuhk	公共事務節目
Publicity Division (GIS)	syùnchyùhnjóu	宣傳組
radio license	gwóngbodihntòih jàpjiu	廣播電台執照
radio pager	mòuhsindihn chyùhnfùgèi	無線電傳呼機
radio with VHF / FM reception	chìudyúnbō tiuhpàhn sàuyàmgèi	超短波調頻收音機
radio-paging	mòuhsindihn chyùhnfù	無線電傳呼
re-boardcast	chùhngbo	重播
re-run programme	chùhngbo jitmuhk	重播節目
relay station	jyúnbojaahm	轉播站
revocation of license	chitsìu pàaihjiu	撤消牌照
royalties	báankyùhn seui	版權稅
serial drama	lìhnjuhk kehkjaap	連續劇集
simulcast	tùhngsìh bofong	同時播放
sound broadcasting	dihntòih gwóngbo	電台廣播
stop press	jeuisàn sìusìk	最新消息
switch stations	jyun tòih	轉台

tele-communica-tion	yúhnchìhng tùngseun	遠程通訊
telecommunica-tions system	mòuhsindihn tùngseunhaihtúng	無線電通訊系統
teletext	dihnsihchyùhnjàn	電視傳真
Television Authority	dihnsihgāamdùk	電視監督
Television Advisory Board	Dihnsih Jìsèun Wáiyùhnwúi	電視諮詢委員會
television critic	dihnsih pìhngleuhnyùhn	電視評論員
television drama	dihnsihkehk	電視劇
television viewer	dihnsih gùnjung	電視觀象
telex	jyùnyuhngdihnbou, yuhngwuhdihnbou	專用電報，用戶電報
the press	sànmàhngaai	新聞界
time slot	jitmuhk bofong sìhgaan	節目播放時間
trailer	yuhgoupín	預告片
transmission/viewing time	bofong sìhgaan	播放時間
up-to-the-minute	jeuisàn	最新
video recording centre	luhkyíng jùngsàm	錄影中心
walkie-talkie	mòuhsindihn tùngwahgèi	無線電通話機
weather report	tìnhei bougou	天氣報告

Magazines	Jaahpji	雜誌
Life	Sàngwuht Jàuhón	生活周刊
National Geographic	Gwokgà Deihléih Yuhthón	國家地理月刊
Newsweek	Sànmàhn Jàuhón	新聞周刊
Playboy	Fāfāgùngjí Yuhthón	花花公子月刊
Reader's Digest	Duhkjé Màhnjaahk	讀者文摘

209

| Time | sìhdoih Jàuhón | 時代周刊 |

News Agency	Tùngseunséh	通訊社
AFP (Agency France-Presse)	Faatsànséh	法新社
AP (Associated Press)	Méihlyùhnséh	美聯社
China News Agency	Jùnggwok Sànmàhnséh	中國新聞社
Reuter (Reuter's News Agency)	Louhtauséh	路透社
TASS (Tele-grafnoie Agent-stvo Sovietskovo Soyuza)	Taapsìséh	塔斯社
UPI (United Press International)	Hahpjung Gwokjai-séh	合衆國際社
Xinhua (New China News Agency)	Sànwàhséh	新華社

Newspapers	boují	報紙
China Daily	Jùnggwok Yahtbou	中國日報
Hong Kong Economic Journal	Seunbou	信報
Hong Kong Tiger Standard	Fúbou	虎報
Ming Pao	Mìhngbou	明報
New York Times	Náuyéuk Sìhbou	紐約時報
Oriental Daily News	Dùngfòng Yahtbou	東方日報
Sing Tao Jih Pao	Sìngdóu Yahtbou	星島日報
South China Morning Post	Nàahmwah jóubou	南華早報
Ta Kung Pao	Daaihgùngbou	大公報

Wah Kiu Yat Pao	Wàhkìuh Yahtbou	華僑日報
Wall Street Journal	Wàhyìhgàai Yahtbou	華爾街日報
Washington Post	Wàhsihngdeuhn Yàuhbou	華盛頓郵報
Wen Wei Po	Màhnwuihbou	文滙報

TV Stations, Radio Stations	Dihnsihtòih, Dihntòih	電視台，電台
Asia Television Broadcasts Ltd.	Ngasih (Ngajàu Dihnsihgwóngbo Yáuhhaahngùngsi)	亞視（亞洲 電視廣播 有限公司）
Chinese channel	Jùngmàhntòih	中文台
Commerical Radio	Sèungyihp Dihntòih	商業電台
English channel	Yìngmàhntòih	英文台
Jade-TVB Chinese Channel	Féicheuitòih	翡翠台
Pearl-TVB English Channel	Mìhngjyùtòih	明珠台
RTHK (Radio Television Hong Kong)	Hèunggóng Dihntòih	香港電台
TVB (H.K. Television Broadcasts Ltd.)	Mòuhsin (Hèunggóng Dihnsih gwóngbo Yáuhhaahngùngsi)	無線（香港 電視廣播 有限公司）

(8) How Hong Kong is run

Government Departments and Secretariat	Jingfú bouhmùhn kahp Boujingsìchyúh	政府部門及布政司署
Agriculture and Fisheries Department	Yùhnùhngchyu	漁農處
Audit Department	Hahtsouchyúh	核數署
Births and Deaths Registries	Sāngséi Jyuchaakchyu	生死註冊處
Census and Statistic Department	Jingfú Túnggaichyu	政府統計處
Civil Aid Services	Màhnjung Ngōnchyùhn Fuhkmouhchyu	民眾安全服務處
Civil Aviation Department	Màhnhòhngchyúh	民航署
Civil Service Branch	Gùngmouhyùhn Chyùhnjeuihfō	公務員銓敍科
Consumer Council	Sìufaijé Wáiyùhnwúi	消費者委員會
Councils and Administration Branch	Hàhngjingfō	行政科
Courts of Justice	Faatyún	法院
District Administration Branch	Deihfònghàhngjingfō	地方行政科
District Council	Kèuiyíhwúi	區議會
Economic Services Branch	Gìngjaifō	經濟科
Education and Manpower Branch	Gaauyuhkkahpyàhnlihk túngchàuhfō	教育及人力統籌科

212

Education Department	Gaauyuhkchyúh	教育署
elected member	màhnsyún yíhyùhn	民選議員
Executive Council	Hàhngjinggúk	行政局
Finance Branch	Chòihjingfō	財政科
Fire Services Department	Siufòhng Sihmouhchyu	消防事務處
Government House	Dūkhinfú	督憲府
Government Information Services	Jingfú Sànmàhnchyu	政府新聞處
Government Laboratory	Jingfú Fayihmsó	政府化驗所
Government Secretariat	Boujingsìchyúh	布政司署
Government Supplies Department	Jingfú Mahtlíu Gùngyingchyu	政府物料供應處
Governor	Góngdūk	港督
Health and Welfare Branch	Séhwúisihmouhfō	社會事務科
Home Affairs Branch	Màhnjingfō	民政科
Home Affairs Department	Màhnjingchyúh	民政署
Housing Branch	Fòhngngūkfō	房屋科
Housing Department	Fòhngngūkchyúh	房屋署
Immigration Department	Yàhnmàhn Yahpgíng Sihmouhchyu	人民入境事務處
Independent Commission Against Corruption	Júngdūk Dahkpaai Lìhmjingjyūnyùhn Gùngchyúh	總督特派廉政專員公署
Inland Revenue Department	Seuimouhgúk	稅務局

Kowloon-Canton Railway	Gáu-Gwóng Titlouhgúk	九廣鐵路局
Labour Department	Lòuhgùngchyu	勞工處
Lands and Works Branch	Deihjinggùngmouhfō	地政工務科
Legal Aid Department	Faatleuhtwùhnjohchyu	法律援助處
Legal Department	Leuhtjingsīchyúh	律政司署
Legislative Council	Lahpfaatgúk	立法局
Marine Department	Hóisihchyu	海事處
Marriage Registries	Fànyàn Jyuchaakchyu	婚姻註冊處
Medical and Health Department	Yìmouhwaihsāngchyu	醫療衛生處
Monetary Affairs Branch	Gàmyùhngsihmouhfō	金融事務科
New Territories Administration	Sàngaai Màhnjingchyúh	新界民政署
official member	gùnsáu yíhyùhn	官守議員
Post Office	Yàuhjingchyúh	郵政署
Printing Department	Jingfú Yanmouhgúk	政府印務局
Prisons Department	Gàamyuhkchyúh	監獄署
Public Enquiry Centres	Jingfú Jìsèunchyu	政府諮詢處
Public Service Commission	Gùngmouhyùhn Jeuihyuhng Wáiyùhnwúi	公務員敍用委員會
Public Works Department	Gùngmouhsìchyúh	工務司署
Radio Television Hong Kong	Hèunggóng Dihntòih	香港電台

Rating and Valuation Department	Chàaihéung Mahtyihp Gúgachyúh	差餉物業估價署
Registrar General's Department	Jyuchaak Júngchyúh	註冊總署
Registration of Persons Office	Yàhnsih Dānggeichyu	人事登記處
Registry of Trade Unions	Jīkgùngwúi Dānggeigúk	職工會登記局
Royal Hong Kong Auxiliary Air Force	Wòhnggā Hèunggóng Fuhjoh Hùnggwàn	皇家香港輔助空軍
Royal Hong Kong Police Force	Wòhnggā Hèunggóng Gìngmouhchyu	皇家香港警務處
Royal Observatory	Tìnmàhntòih	天文台
Security Branch	Bóungònfò	保安科
Social Welfare Department	Séhwúifūkleihchyúh	社會福利署
Television and Entertainment Licensing Authority	Yíngsih kahp Yùhlohksihmouh Gúnléihchyu	影視及娛樂事務管理處
The Attorney General	Leuhtjingsī	律政司
The Chief Secretary	Boujingsī	布政司
The Commander British Forces	Jyugóng Yìnggwàn Júngsīlihng	駐港英軍總司令
The Financial Secretary	Chòihjingsī	財政司
The Secretary for District Administration	Deihjingsī	地政司
The Secretary for Home Affairs	Màhnjingsī	政務司

Trade and Industry Branch	Gùngsèungfō	工商科
Trade Industry and Customs Department	Gùngsèungchyúh	工商署
Transport Branch	Wahnsyūfō	運輸科
Transport Department	Wahnsyūchyu	運輸處
Treasury Department	Fumouhchyúh	庫務署
University and Polytechnic Grants Committee (U.P.G.C)	Daaihhohk kahp Léihgùng Gaauyuhk Jìjoh Wáiyùhnwúi	大學及理工教育資助委員會
unofficial member	fèigùnsáu yíhyùhn	非官守議員
Urban Council and Urban Services Department	Sìhjinggúk kahp Sìhjing-sihmouhchyúh	市政局及市政事務署

(9) Where to worship in Hong Kong

Churches and Temples	Gaautòhng kahp Muiyúh	教堂及廟宇
Che Kung Temple	Chègùng Míu	車公廟
Chinese Baptist Church	Jamseunwúi Tòhng	浸信會堂
Chinese Methodist Church (on H.K. side)	Jùngwàh Chèuhndouh Gùngwúi	中華循道公會
Chinese Methodist Church (on Kowloon side)	Jùngwàh Chèuhndouhwúi	中華循道會
Ching Chung Koon Temple	Chìngchùhng Gun	青松觀
Ching Leung Fat Yuen Temple	Chìnglèuhng Faatyún	清涼法苑
Chuk Lam Sim Yuen Temple	Jùklàhm Sìhmyún	竹林禪院
Confucius Hall	Húngsing Tòhng	孔聖堂
Fung Ying Sin Koon Temple	Fùhngyìhng Sìngún	蓬瀛仙館
Hau Wong Temple	Hàuhwòhng Míu	侯皇廟
Hop Yat Church	Hahpyāt Tòhng	合一堂
Immaculate Heart of Mary's Church	Daaihbou Tìnjyútòhng	大埔天主堂
Kowloon Mosque	Gáulùhng Wùihgaaumíu	九龍回教廟
Kun 'um Temple	Gùnyàm Míu	觀音廟
Kung Lee Church	Gùngléih Tòhng	公理堂
Living Spirit Lutheran Church	Seunyihwúi Wuhtlìhngtòhng	信義會活靈堂
Man Mo Temple	Màhnmóuh Míu	文武廟

Moslem Mosque	Wùihgaau Láihbaai-tòhng	回教禮拜堂
Pentecostal Church	Ńghchèuhnjit Tòhng	五旬節堂
Roman Catholic Cathedral	Tìnjyúgaau Júngtòhng	天主教總堂
Rosary Church	Mùihgwai Tòhng	玫瑰堂
Sam Shing Temple	Sàamsing Míu	三聖廟
Sihh Temple	Yandouh Míu	印度廟
St. Andrew's Church	Singngòndākliht Tòhng	聖安德烈堂
St. Francis of Assisi's Church	Singfòngjaigok Tòhng	聖方濟各堂
St. John's Cathedral	Singyeukhohn Daaihgaautòhng	聖約翰大教堂
St. Joseph's Church	Singyeuksāt Tòhng	聖約瑟堂
St. Mary's Church	Singmáhleihnga Tòhng	聖瑪利亞堂
St. Paul's Church	Singbóulòh Tòhng	聖保羅堂
St. Teresa's Church	Singdāklaahksaat Tòhng	聖德肋撒堂
Temple of 10,000 Buddhas	Maahnfaht Jí	萬佛寺
Tin Hau Temple	Tìnhauh Míu	天后廟
Truth Lutheran Church	Jànléih Tòhng	眞理堂
Tsing Shan Tsz Temple	Chìngsàan Ji	青山寺
Tung Po To Temple	Dùngpóutòh	東普陀
Union Church	Yauhlìhng Tòhng	祐寧堂
Wong Tai Sin Temple	Wòhngdaaihsìn Míu	黃大仙廟
Yuen Yuen Hok Yuen Temple	Yùhnyùhn Hohkyún	圓玄學院

(10) How education is conducted

academic / educational qualifications	hohklihk	學歷
academic achievement	hohkyihp sìhngjik	學業成績
Academic Aptitude Test (A.A.T.)	Hohkyihpnàhnglihk Chāakyihm	學業能力測驗
academic board	haauhmouh wáiyùhnwúi	校務委員會
academic secretary / registrar	gaaumouhjéung	教務長
academic year	hohknìhn	學年
accomplishment test	geihnàhn chāakyihm	技能測驗
acheivement test	sìhngjik chàakyihm	成績測驗
activity approach	wuhtduhng gaauhohkfaat	活動教學法
admission of pupils	chéuiluhk hohksàng	取錄學生
Adult Education and Recreation Centre	Sìhngyàhn Gaauyuhk Hònglohk Jùngsàm	成人教育康樂中心
adult education	sìhngyàhn gaauyuhk	成人教育
Advanced Level Examination of the University of Hong Kong	Gòukáp Chìhngdouh Háausìh	高級程度考試
aided school	jìjoh hohkhaauh	資助學校
Alliance Francaise	Faatgwok Màhnfa Hipwúi	法國文化協會
allocation slip	paaiwáijing	派位證
alumni	haauhyáuh	校友

Anglo-Chinese secondary grammar school	yingmàhn màhnfaat jùnghohk	英文文法中學
application form	sànchingbíu	申請表
appointment service	jikyihp fuhdouhchyu	職業輔導處
apprenticeship	hohktòuhjai	學徒制
aptitude test	hohknàhng chāakyihm	學能測驗
Area Inspectorate	Fànkèui Sihhohkchyu	分區視學處
art and craft teacher	méih-lòuh gaausì	美勞教師
arts	màhnfò	文科
attendance register	dímméngbóu	點名簿
Audio-visual Education Section	Sihting Gaauyuhkjóu	視聽教育組
audio-visual aid	sihting gaaugeuih	視聽教具
bazaar	maaihmahtwúi	賣物會
behavioural psychology	hàhngwàih sàmléihhohk	行爲心理學
Beijing-Hong Kong Academic Exchange Centre	Gìng-Góng Hohkseuht Gàaulàuh Jùngsàm	京港學術交流中心
bi-sessional school	bunyahtjai hohkhaauh	半日制學校
block subsidy	dihngngáak jèuntip	定額津貼
Board of Education	Gaauyuhk Wáiyùhnwúi	教育委員會
bookstock	tòuhsyù chòhngleuhng	圖書藏量
British Council	Yinggwok Màhnfa Hipwúi	英國文化協會
Business Studies	Sèungyihphohk	商業學
C.U.H.K. (The Chinese University of Hong Kong)	Jùng daaih (Jùngmàhndaaihhohk)	中大（中文大學）

cafeteria	chàantèng	餐廳
canteen	faahntòhng	飯堂
capital / building grant	ginhaauh jèuntip	建校津貼
Certificate in Education (Cert. Ed.)	Gaauyuhk Jingsyù	教育證書
Certificate of Education Examination	Jùnghohk Wuihháau	中學會考
Certificate of Education	Wuihháau jingsyù	會考證書
Certificated Master / Mistress (C.M.)	màhnpàhng gaausì	文憑教師
Chancellor (H.K.U. and C.U.)	Haauhgàam	校監
Child Care Centre	Yauyìh Jùngsàm	幼兒中心
Chinese middle school	Jùngmàhn jùnghohk	中文中學
Chung Chi College	Sùhnggèi Hohkyún	崇基學院
civic education	gùngmàhn gaauyuhk	公民教育
college of education	sifaahn hohkyún	師範學院
commercial and secretarial program	sèungfò kahp beisyù fochìhng	商科及秘書課程
complementary education	fuhjoh gaauyuhk	輔助教育
compulsory education	kèuhngbìk gaauyuhk	强迫教育
compulsory school attendance	kèuhngbìk yahphohk	强迫入學
computer program	dihnnóuh fochìhng	電腦課程
cooking class	pàangyahm bàan	烹飪班

221

correspondence program	hàahmsauh fochìhng	函授課程
course	hohkfò	學科
course number	fochìhng pìnhouh	課程編號
crash course	chūksìhng fochìhng	速成課程
credit	hohkfàn	學分
curricular activity	fosàt wuhtduhng	課室活動
curriculum guides	fochìhng jínàahm	課程指南
day nursery	yahtgàan yauyìh jùngsàm	日間幼兒中心
degree	hohkwái	學位
degree examination	hohkwáisìh	學位試
Degree of Doctor of Laws, honoris causa	wìhngyuh faathohk boksih hohkwái	榮譽法學博士學位
demonstration room	sihfaahn sāt	示範室
Department of Extramural Studies	haauhngoih jeunsàubouh	校外進修部
Diploma in Education	gaauyuhk màhnpàhng	教育文憑
Director of Education	Gaauyuhkchyúh Chyúhjéung	教育署署長
discipline master	fandouh jyúyahm	訓導主任
dismissal of pupils	hòichèuih hohksàang	開除學生
drop a course	teuisàu	退修
drop-out	jùngtòuh teuihohk hohksàang	中途退學學生
duration of course	sàuyihp kèihhaahn	修業期限
education allowance	gaauyuhk jèuntip	教育津貼

education counselling	gaauyuhk fuhdouh	教育輔導
Education Commission	Gaauyuhktúngcháuh Wáiyùhnwúi	教育統籌委員會
Education Scholarships Fund Committee	Gaauyuhk Jéunghohkgàm Wáiyùhnwúi	教育獎學金委員會
Education Officer	Gaauyuhkgùn	教育官
Education Department	Gaauyuhkchyúh	教育署
education institution	gaauyuhk gèikau	教育機構
Education Ordinance	Gaauyuhk Tìuhlaih	教育條例
Education Television (E.T.V.)	Gaauyuhk Dihnsih	教育電視
educational psychology	gaauyuhk sàmléihhohk	教育心理學
educational value	gaauyuhk gajihk	教育價值
elite education	jìngyìng gaauyuhk	精英教育
enrol	yahpduhk	入讀
entry qualification / requirement	yahpphohk jìgaak	入學資格
estate school	gùngguhng ngùkchyùn hohkhaauh	公共屋村學校
evening courses	máahngàan fochìhng	晚間課程
evening school	yehhaauh	夜校
examination system	háausíh jaidouh	考試制度
Examination Division	Háausíh Jóu	考試組
exchange student	gàauwuhnsàng	交換生
extended day system	yìhnchèuhngyaht jai	延長日制
external degree	haauhngoih hohkwái	校外學位

223

external examinations	hóingoih háausíh	校外考試
extra-curricular activity	fongoih wuhtduhng	課外活動
faculty	hohkyún	學院
five-year-course school	ńghnihnjai jùnghohk	五年制中學
floatation / floating class	fàuhduhngbāan	浮動班
free education	mihnfai gaauyuhk	免費教育
full-time course	chyùhnyahtjai fochìhng	全日制課程
full-time teacher	jyúnyahm gaausí	專任教師
further education	sàmchou	深造
games day	yàuhheiyaht	游戲日
general education	tùngchòih gaauyuhk	通才教育
good honours degree	daaihhohk gòukàp wihngyuh hohkwái	大學高級榮譽學位
government secondary school	gùnlahp jùnghohk	官立中學
government school	gùnlahp hohkhaauh (gùnhaauh)	官立學校（官校）
grade point average (G.P.A.)	pìhnggwàn jikdím	平均積點
grade report	sìhngjikbíu	成績表
grant school	bóujoh jùnghohk	補助中學
Grantham Training College	Gotleuhnghùhng Sìfaahn Hohkyún	葛量洪師範學院
H.K.U. (University of Hong Kong)	Góng daaih (Hèunggóng daaihhohk)	港大（香港大學）
handicapped children	yeuhknáhng yìhtùhng	弱能兒童
health center	bóugihnchyu	保健處
higher education	gòudáng gaauyuhk	高等教育

Higher Level Examination of the Chinese University of Hong Kong	Gòudáng Chìhngdouh Háausih	高等程度考試
Hong Kong Association for Continuing Education	Hèunggóng Sìhngyàhn Gaauyuhk Hipwúi	香港成人教育協會
Hong Kong Technical Teacher's College	Hèunggóng Gùngsèung Sìfaahn hohkyún	香港工商師範學院
Hong Kong Examinations Authority	Hèunggóng Háausìhgúk	香港考試局
Hong Kong Teacher's Association	Hèunggóng Gaausìwúi	香港教師會
Hong Kong Training Council	Hèunggóng Fanlihngúk	香港訓練局
Hong Kong Polytechnic	Hèunggóng Léihgùng Hohkyún	香港理工學院
Hong Kong Academy for Performing Arts	Hèunggóng Yínngaih Hohkyún	香港演藝學院
Hong Kong Baptist College	Jamwúi Hohkyún	浸會學院
Hong Kong Children's Choir	Hèunggóng Yìhtùhng Hahpcheungtyùhn	香港兒童合唱團
Hong Kong City Polytechnic	Hèunggóng Sìhngsìh Léihgùng Hohkyún	香港城市理工學院
Hong Kong Federation of Education Workers	Hèunggóng Gaauyuhkgùngjokjé Lyùhnwúi	香港教育工作者聯會
Hong Kong International School	Hèunggóng Gwokjaihohkhaauh	香港國際學校

Hong Kong Schools Music Festival	Hèunggóng Haauhjai Yàmngohkjit	香港校際音樂節
Hong Kong Sea School	Hèunggóng Hòhnhói Hohkhaauh	香港航海學校
honours degree	wìhngyuh hohkwái	榮譽學位
in-service re-training	joihjik gaausì fuksàu fanlihn	在職教師複修訓練
Inspector	dùkhohk	督學
Institute of International Education	Gwokjai Gaauyuhk Hipwúi	國際教育協會
Institute of Language in Education	Yùhmàhn Gaauyuhk Hohkyún	語文教育學院
intelligence quotient (IQ)	jisèung	智商
internship	sahtjaahp	實習
interview	mihnsíh	面試
invigilation	gàamháau	監考
junior English school	Yìngtùhng Síuhohk	英童小學
laboratory technician	sahtyihmsāt geihseuhtyùhn	實驗室技術員
laboratory	sahtyihmsāt	實驗室
language laboratory	yúhyìhn sahtjaahpsāt	語言實習室
language program	yúhyìhn fochìhng	語言課程
language skill	yúhyìhn geihháau	語言技巧
liberal arts	daaihhohk màhnfò	大學文科
Lingnan College	Lìhngnàahm Syùyún	嶺南書院
listening comprehension	tinglihk léihgáai	聽力理解
major subjects	jyúsàu fōmuhk	主修科目
maladjusted and socially deprived children	chìhngsèuihmahntàih hohksàang	情緒問題學生

master / mistress (of the class)	bàanjyúyahm	班主任
matriculation	daaihhohk yuhfō	大學預科
matriculation course	yuhfōbàan	預科班
mature student	chiulìhng hohksàang	超齡學生
medium of instruction	gaauhohk yúhyìhn	教學語言
microfilm	hínmèih gàaugyún	顯微膠卷
minor staff	haauhgùng	校工
New Asia College	Sànnga Syùyún	新亞書院
New Asia-Yale-in-China Chinese Language Center	Sànngáh Jùnggwok Yúhmàhn Yìhn-jaahpsó	新雅中國語文研習所
nine years of general educa-tion for all	gáunìhn póukahp gaauyuhk	九年普及教育
nine-year subsi-dized primary and secondary education	gáunìhn jùngsíuhohk jìjoh gaauyuhk	九年中小學資助教育
non-graduate teacher	fèihohkwái gaausì	非學位教師
non-profit-making private secon-dary school	fèimàuhleih sìlahp jùnghohk	非牟利私立中學
Northcote Training College	Lòhfugwok Sìfaahn Hohkhaauh	羅富國師範學院
open day	hòifong yaht	開放日
open university	gùnghòi daaihhohk	公開大學
orientation course	sìndouh fochìhng	先導課程
outdoor education camp	wuhngoih gaauyuhk yìhng	戶外教育營
outward bound courses	ngoihjín fanlihn fochìhng	外展訓練課程

parent-teacher association	gaausi-gàjéung wúi	教師家長會
parents day	gàjéung yaht	家長日
part-time degree program	gimduhk hohkwái fochìhng	兼讀學位課程
part-time teacher	gìmyahm gaausì	兼任教師
post-secondary college	jyùnseuhng hohkyún (daaihjyùn)	專上學院（大專）
pre-vocational school	jikyihpsinsàu hohkhaauh	職業先修學校
presenter (E.T.V.)	dihnsih gaausì	電視教師
private post-secondary colleges	daaihjyùn hohkyún	大專學院
private school	sìlahp hohkhaauh (sìhaauh)	私立學校（私校）
private tutorial school	bóujaahp hohkhaauh	補習學校
Professional Teachers' Union	Hèunggóng Gaauyuhk Yàhnyùhn Jyùnyihp Hipwúi	香港教育人員專業協會
professional education	jyùnyihp gaauyuhk	專業教育
programme	fochìhng	課程
public examination	gùnghòi háausíh	公開考試
pupil-teacher ratio	hohksàang yùh gaausì béiléut	學生與教師比率
quiz competition	mahndaap béichoi	問答比賽
Recreation and Sport Service (R.S.S.)	Hònglohk Táiyuhk Sihmouhchyu (Hòngtáichyu)	康樂體育事務處（康體處）
refresher training	fùksàubàan	複修班
registered teacher	gímdihng gaausì	檢定教師

228

registrar of the university	daaihhohk jyuchaak jyúyahm	大學註冊主任
religious institution	jùnggaau gèikau	宗教機構
residential course	jyuhsùk fochìhng	住宿課程
sandwich course / programme	gàautaijai fochìhng	交替制課程
scholarship	jéunghohkgàm	獎學金
School Dance Festival	Hohkhaauh Móuhdouhjit	學校舞蹈節
school fee, tuition	hohkfai	學費
School Medical Service Scheme	Hohksàang Bóugihngaiwaahk	學生保健計劃
School of Education	Gaauyuhk Hohkyún	教育學院
school road safety patrol	hohkhaauh gàautùng-ngònchyùhndéui	學校交通安全隊
school social worker	hohkhaauh sèhwúigùngjokjé	學校社會工作者
School Social Work Scheme	Hohkhaauh sèhwúigùngjok gaiwaahk	學校社會工作計劃
school uniform	haauhfuhk	校服
seaman training centre	hóiyùhn fanlihn jùngsàm	海員訓練中心
seminar	yìhntóuwúi	研討會
Senate (H.K.U. and C.U.H.K.)	Daaihhohk Gaaumouhwúi	大學教務會
serving teacher	joihjìk gaauyùhn	在職教員
sex education	sing gaauyuhk	性教育
Shue Yan College	Syuhyàhn Syúyún	樹仁書院
Sir Robert Black Training College	Paaklaahpgèi Sìfaahn Hohkyún	柏立基師範學院
special education	dahksyùh gaauyuhk	特殊教育
speech day	bàanjéung yaht	頒獎日

speech therapy	yìhnyúh jihlìuh	言語治療
split classes	fànfò séuhngfo bàankàp	分科上課班級
sports center	táiyuhk jùngsàm	體育中心
staff	gaaujìkyùhn	教職員
student assembly	hohksàang jaahpwúi	學生集會
student guidance scheme	hohksàang fuhdouhgaiwaahk	學生輔導計劃
student intake	jìusàu hohksàang yàhnsou	招收學生人數
student subculture	hohksàang hyùnnoihmàhnfa	學生圈內文化
Subject Officer	fòmuhk jyúyahm	科目主任
subject-oriented teaching	hohkfòwàihbún gaauhohk	學科爲本教學
subsidised school	jèuntip hohkhaauh	津貼學校
substitute / supply teacher	doihfo gaausì	代課教師
summer recreation programme	syúkèih hònglohkwuhtduhng	暑期康樂活動
summer vacation	syúga	暑假
supervisor	haauhgàam	校監
swimming gala, aquatic meet	séuiwahnwúi	水運會
syllabus	fochìhng gòngyiu	課程綱要
symposium	jyùntàih yìhntóuwúi	專題研討會
take school bus	daap haauh bà	搭校巴
taped programme	luhkyàm gaauchòih	錄音教材
teachers' centre	gaausì jùngsàm	教師中心
teaching aids	gaauyuhk heichòih	教育器材
teaching block	haauhse	校舍
team teaching	kwàhntái gaauhohk	羣體教學
technical institute	gùngyihp hohkhaauh	工業學校
technical teacher	gùngyihp gaausì	工業教師
terms of reference	jìkkyùhn faahnwàih	職權範圍

230

tertiary education	jyùnseuhng gaauyuhk	專上教育
The Chinese University of Hong Kong (C.U.H.K.)	Hèunggóng Jùngmàhn Daaihhohk (Jùngdaaih)	香港中文大學 （中大）
The University of Hong Kong (H.K.U.)	Hèunggóng Daaihhohk (Góngdaaih)	香港大學（港大）
three-year bought place scheme	sàamnìhnjai kaumáaih hohkwái gaiwaahk	三年制購買學位計劃
training course	fanlihn fochìhng	訓練課程
truancy	tòuhhohk	逃學
tutorial class	douhsàubàan	導修班
U.P.G.C. (University and Polytechnic Grants Committee)	Daaihhohk kahp Léihgùng gaauyuhk buhtfún Wáiyùhnwúi	大學及理工教育撥款委員會
unitary system	túngyàtjai	統一制
United College	Lyùhnhahp Syùyún	聯合書院
unruly behaviour	faahnkwài hàhngwàih	犯規行為
Vice-Chancellor (H.K.U. and C.U.)	haauhjéung	校長
visual arts education	sihgok ngaihseuht gaauyuhk	視覺藝術教育
vocational training	jikyihp fanlihn	職業訓練
vocational guidance	jikyihp fuhdouh	職業輔導
what is (your) major?	duhk matyeh haih	讀乜嘢系
winter vacation	hòhnga	寒假
work camp	gùngjok yìhng	工作營
workshop	yìhnjaahpbàan	研習班

Appendices

Family relations	Chànsuhk Chìngwaih	親屬稱謂
aunt	baakleùhng (wife of father's elder brothers)	伯娘
aunt	gūmà (father's elder sister)	姑媽
aunt	gūjè (father's younger sister)	姑姐
aunt	yìhmā (mother's elder sister)	姨媽
aunt	káuhmóuh, káhmmóuh (wife of mother's brother)	舅姆，妗姆
aunt	asám (wife of father's younger brother)	阿嬸
aunty	ayì (mother's younger sister)	阿姨
aunty	ayì, yìyì (general term)	阿姨，姨姨
brothers	hìngdaih	兄弟
brother-in-law	jéfù (husband of one's elder sister)	姐夫
brother-in-law	muihfù (husband of one's younger sister)	妹夫
brother-in-law	daaihkáuh (elder brother of one's wife)	大舅

brother-in-law	káuhjái (younger brother of one's wife)	舅仔
brother-in-law	daaihbaak (elder brother of one's husband)	大伯
brother-in-law	sūkjái (younger brother of one's husband)	叔仔
cousin	tòhngagō (elder male on father's side)	堂阿哥
cousin	tòhng sailóu (younger male on father's side)	堂細佬
cousin	tòhnggājè (elder female on father's side)	堂家姐
cousin	tòhngsaimúi (younger female on father's side)	堂細妹
cousin	bíujé (elder female on mother's side)	表姐
cousin	bíumúi (younger female on mother's side)	表妹
cousin	bíugò (elder male on mother's side)	表哥
cousin	bíudài (younger male on mother's side)	表弟
daughter	néui	女
daughter-in-law	sànpóuh	新抱
elder brother	gòhgō, daaihlóu	哥哥, 大佬
elder sister	gajē, jèhjè	家姐, 姐姐
father	bàhbā, a bàh, fuhchàn	爸爸, 阿爸, 父親

father-in-law	ngoihfú, ngohkfú (father of one's wife)	外父,岳父
father-in-law	lóuhyèh (father of one's husband)	老爺
grand-daughter	syùnnéui (daughter of one's son)	孫女
grand-daughter	ngoihsyùnnéui (daughter of one's daughter)	外孫女
grandfather	yèhyé, a yèh (on father's side)	爺爺,阿爺
grandfather	gùnggùng, ngoihgùng, a gùng (on mother's side)	公公,外公,阿公
grandmother	màhmàh, a màh (on father's side)	嬤嬤,阿嬤
grandmother	pòhpó, ngoihpòh, a pòh (on mother's side)	婆婆,外婆,阿婆
grandson	syùn (son of one's son)	孫
grandson	ngoihsyùn (son of one's daughter)	外孫
husband	jeuhngfu, lóuhgùng, sìnsàang	丈夫,老公,先生
mother	màhmà, a mā, móuhchàn	媽媽,阿媽,母親
mother-in-law	nàaihnáai, gāpó (mother of one's husband)	奶奶,家婆
mother-in-law	ngoihmóu, ngohkmóu (mother of one's wife)	外母,岳母
nephew	jàt (son of one's brother)	侄

nephew	ngoihsàng (son of one's sister)	外甥
niece	jahtnéui (daughter of one's brother)	侄女
niece	ngoihsàngnéui (daughter of one's sister)	外甥女
sister-in-law	a sóu (wife of one's elder brother)	阿嫂
sister-in-law	daihfúh (wife of one's younger brother)	弟婦
sister-in-law	daaihyìh (elder sister of one's wife)	大姨
sister-in-law	yijái (younger sister of one's wife)	姨仔
sister-in-law	gùnāai (elder sister of one's husband)	姑奶
sister-in-law	gùjái (younger sister of one's husband)	姑仔
sisters	jímuih	姊妹
son	jai	仔
son-in-law	néuihsai	女婿
uncle	a baak, baakfuh (elder brother of one's father)	阿伯, 伯父
uncle	a sūk, sūkfuh (younger brother of one's father)	阿叔, 叔父
uncle	gùjéung (husband of a sister of one's father)	姑丈

uncle	yìhjéung (husband of a sister of one's mother)	姨丈
uncle	káuhfú, káauhfú (brother of one's mother)	舅父
uncle	sūksùk (general term)	叔叔
wife	taaitáai. lóuhpòh, chàijí	太太、老婆、妻子
younger brother	dàihdái, sailóu	弟弟、細佬
younger sister	mùihmúi, saimúi	妹妹、細妹

"Loanwords" in Cantonese

Ngoihlòihyúh   外來語

Amen	amùhn, amaahng	阿門, 阿孟
Arrow-shirt	ālóusēut	鴉佬恤
baby	bìhbì	啤啤
ball	bō	波
ballet	balèuihmóuh	芭蕾舞
band	bēng	□
beer	bējáu	啤酒
boss	bōsí	波士
bowling	bóulìhngkàuh	保齡球
boxing	bōksíng	□□
boycott	bùigot	杯葛
Brandy	bahtlāandéi	白蘭地
bus	bāsí	巴士
bye bye	bāaibaai	拜拜
cancer	kènsá	□□
card	kāat	卡
cartoon	kàtùng	卡通
cash	kèsyùh	□□
cashmere	kèsihmē	茄士咩

236

catsup	kéjāp	茄汁
certificate	sàjí	沙紙
Charlie (Chaplin)	chāléi	差利
check	chēk	□
cheese	jìsí	芝士
cheque	chēk	仄
chocolate	jyùgūlìk	朱古力
cigar	syutgā	雪茄
club	kèuilohkbouh	俱樂部
cocktail	gàiméihjáu	鷄尾酒
cocoa	gūkgú	哈咕
coffee	gafē	咖啡
cookie	kùkkèih	曲奇
coolie	gùlēi	□□
cream soda	geihlìmsōdá	忌廉梳打
curry	galēi	咖喱
daddy	dèdìh	爹哋
darling	dālìng	打令
dozen	dā	打
duce	diusìh	刁時
fail	fèihlóu	肥佬
file, holder	fàailóu	快勞
film	fèilám	菲林
gallon	gāléun	加侖
Gin	jinjáu	氈酒
golf	gòyìhfùkàuh	高爾夫球
guitar	gittā	結他
hot dog	yihtgáu	熱狗
humour	yàumahk	幽默
jam	gwójīm	菓占
James Bond	jimsihbòng	占士邦
Jazz	jeuksihyàmngohk	爵士音樂
jelly	jēléi	啫喱
lemon	lìhngmùng	檸檬
lift	līp	□
mammy	māmìh	媽咪
mango	mònggwó	芒果

237

mark	māak	嘜
Martini	màhtìnnèih	馬天尼
meter	māibiu	咪錶
microphone	māi	咪
mile	māi	咪
milk shake	nàaihsīk	奶昔
mince	mìhnjih	免治
mini	màihnèih	迷你
Miss	mītsih	□□
model	mòuhdahkyìh	模特兒
modern	mōdàng	摩登
motor	mōdá	摩打
name card	kāatpín	卡片
nylon	nàih(nèih)lùhng	尼龍
ounce	ōnsí	安士
Ovatine	òwàhtìhn	阿華田
pair	pē	□
pan cake	bāankīk	班戟
partner	pāatnàh	□□
pass(examination)	pāsìh	□□
passport	pāsihpòt	□□□
pear	bēléi	啤梨
pie	pài	批
Ping Pong	bīngbāmbò	乒乓波
port (wine)	būtjáu	砵酒
postcard	pòusìhkāat	甫士咭
Potassium Cyanide	sàan(ng)àai	山埃
pound	bohng	磅
pudding	boudīn	布甸
quarter	gwāt	骨
radar	lèuihdaaht	雷達
salad	sàléut	沙律
Salmon	sàammàhnyú	三文魚
shirt	sèutsàam	恤衫
Sir	asèuh	啊蛇
size	sāaisí	晒士
sofa	sòfá	梳化

saamahnji = Sandwich

solo	sōulòuh	□□
spare	sihbē	士啤
stamp	sihdāam	士担
store	sihdò	士多
strawberry	sihdōbēléi	士多啤梨
Sunkist	sànkèihsih	新奇士
tank	táanhāak	坦克
tart	daahntāat	蛋撻
taxi	dīksí	的士
Terylene	dahkleihlìhng	特麗令
tie	tāai	呔
tips	tipsí	貼士
toast	dòsí	多士
toffee	tòféitóng	拖肥糖
ton	dèun	噸
tyre	tāai	□
Vitamin	wàihtàmìhng	維他命
Waffle	wāifabéng	威化餅
Waltz	wàhyíhjì	華爾滋
Whisky	wāisihgéi	威士忌
X-ray	īksìhgwòng	X光

light (or right)

Twelve animal signs of the Chinese Zodiac (year)	Sahpyih Sàngchiu	十二生肖

life, birth   look like

Rat	Syú	鼠
Ox	Ngàuh	牛
Tiger	Fú	虎
Rabbit	Tou	兔
Dragon	Lùhng	龍
Snake	Sèh	蛇
Horse	Máh	馬
Sheep	Yèuhng	羊
Monkey	Hàuh	猴

fook = fortune
foorsyú = fortune roll

239

Rooster	Gài	鶏
Dog	Gáu	狗
Boar	Jyù	猪

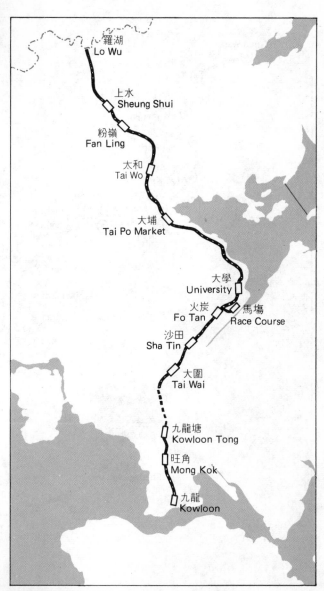

KCR See pp. 139-140

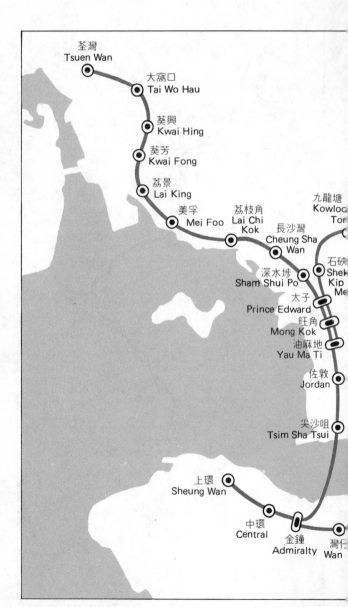

MTR See pp. 138-139

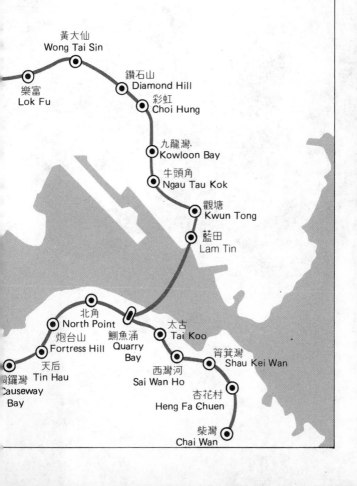

黃大仙
Wong Tai Sin

鑽石山
Diamond Hill

彩虹
Choi Hung

樂富
Lok Fu

九龍灣
Kowloon Bay

牛頭角
Ngau Tau Kok

觀塘
Kwun Tong

藍田
Lam Tin

北角
North Point

鰂魚涌
Quarry
Bay

太古
Tai Koo

炮台山
Fortress Hill

天后
Tin Hau

西灣河
Sai Wan Ho

筲箕灣
Shau Kei Wan

銅鑼灣
Causeway
Bay

杏花村
Heng Fa Chuen

柴灣
Chai Wan